LEARN TO PAINT WITH
WATERCOLOURS
ALWYN CRAWSHAW FRSA

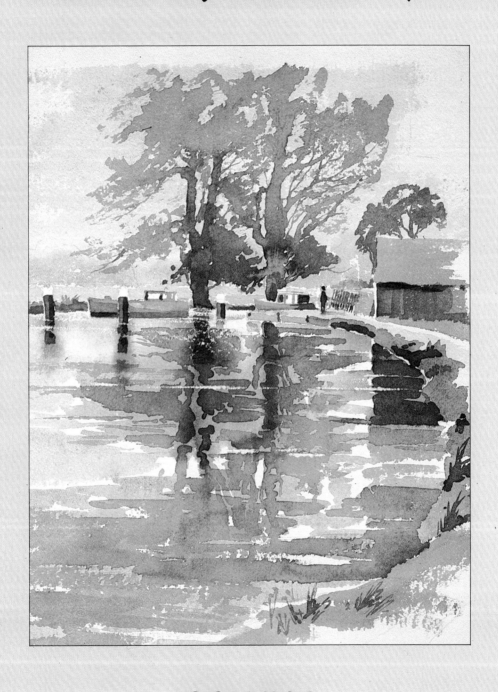

COLLINS
GLASGOW & LONDON

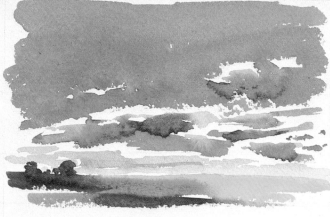

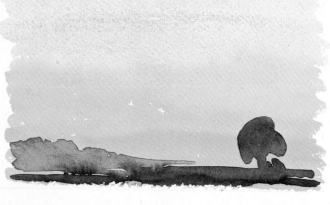

First published 1979
Collins Publishers, Glasgow and London

© Alwyn Crawshaw 1979

Designed and edited by Youé and Spooner Limited
Filmset by Tradespools Limited
Colour processing by Medway Reprographic Limited
Photography by Michael Petts

ISBN 0 00 411870 7

Printed in Great Britain

Rowney brushes and Artists' Quality Water Colours were used for
all the paintings illustrated in this book. Alwyn Crawshaw uses
these colours for all his watercolour paintings and finds their
consistency and permanence incomparable.

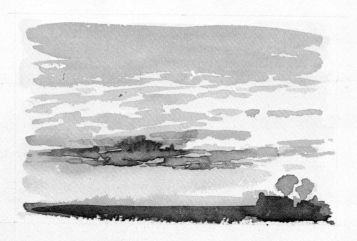

CONTENTS

PORTRAIT OF AN ARTIST ALWYN CRAWSHAW *FRSA*

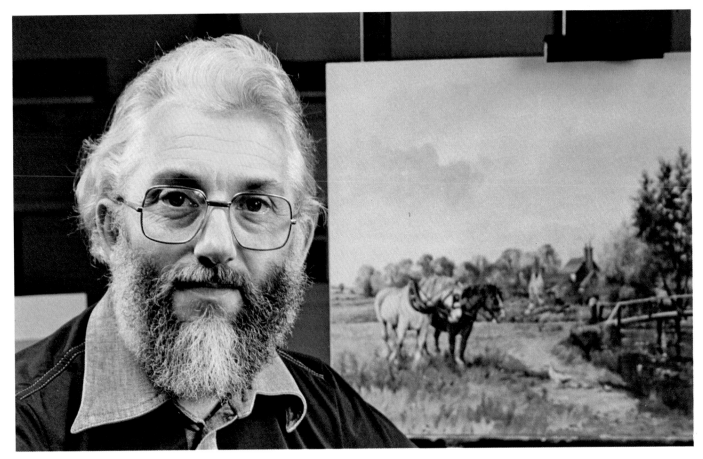

Alwyn Crawshaw was born in 1934 at Mirfield, Yorkshire: he now lives in Surrey. During his earlier years, he studied the many facets of watercolour and oil painting and, more recently, acrylic painting. Now a successful painter, author and lecturer, his work has brought him recognition as one of the leading authorities in his field.

Crawshaw paints what he terms realistic subjects and these include many English landscape scenes which are frequently the subject of favourable articles and reviews by the critics. In most of Crawshaw's landscapes there can be found a distinctive 'trade-mark' – usually elm trees or working horses.

The widespread popularity of Alwyn Crawshaw's work developed after his painting, *Wet and Windy*, had been included among the top ten prints chosen by the members of the Fine Art Trade Guild in 1975. Fine art prints of this well known painting are still very much in demand throughout the world. Another now famous painting was completed during Queen Elizabeth's Jubilee Year in 1977 when Crawshaw felt that he would like to record a particular

aspect of the heritage of Britain symbolised by the celebrations of that year. After lengthy and painstaking research and hours spent working at the location, Crawshaw completed *The Silver Jubilee Fleet Review 1977*. Crawshaw has been a guest on the *Jack de Manio Precisely* radio programme where he discussed his painting techniques. He demonstrates these techniques to members of many art societies throughout the country.

Many of Crawshaw's paintings are dispersed throughout the world. They are sold in art galleries in the main centres of the United Kingdom, France, Germany, North and South America, Australia and Scandinavia. Some of his works have also been exhibited in Russia and in Eastern Europe, particularly Poland, Hungary and Romania.

Among some of the most important one-man exhibitions of Crawshaw's work are his three shows in the art gallery at Harrods, the famous department store in Knightsbridge, London. He also held a one-man exhibition at Chester, which was opened by the Duchess of Westminster who now has a Crawshaw painting in her private collection.

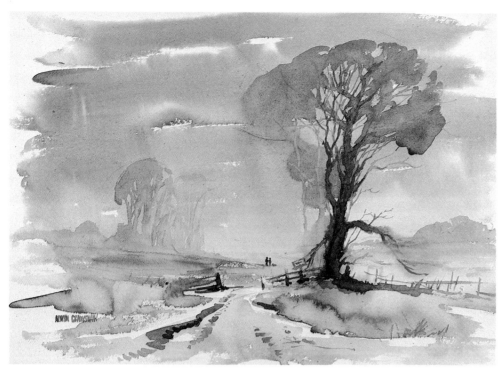

Between the showers, 45.7 × 34cm (18 × 13⅜in). Private collection, London

One-man shows of his work frequently draw an enthusiastic audience, no doubt because his paintings are popular with both public and critics alike. There is a feeling of reality about them, an atmosphere which at times succeeds in transmitting to the onlooker a faint memory, as if one had been there before. Whatever it is, and no matter the season of the year, this feeling is usually experienced wherever Crawshaw's paintings are on view.

Alwyn Crawshaw is married and he and his wife have three children, two teenage daughters and a younger son. At weekends or holidays a sketching day will frequently turn into a family day out.

According to Alwyn Crawshaw, there are two attributes necessary for success as an artist: dedication and a sense of humour. The need for the first is self evident; the second 'helps you out of many a crisis'. In addition, Crawshaw acknowledges the unfailing loyalty of his wife and family.

Home to the farm, 64 × 35.5cm (24 × 14in). Author's collection

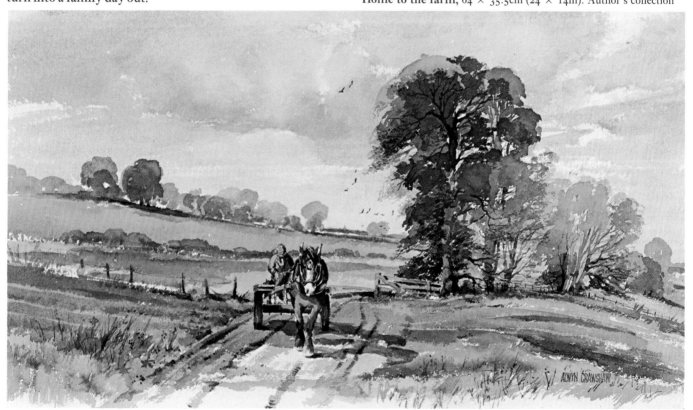

WHY PAINT?

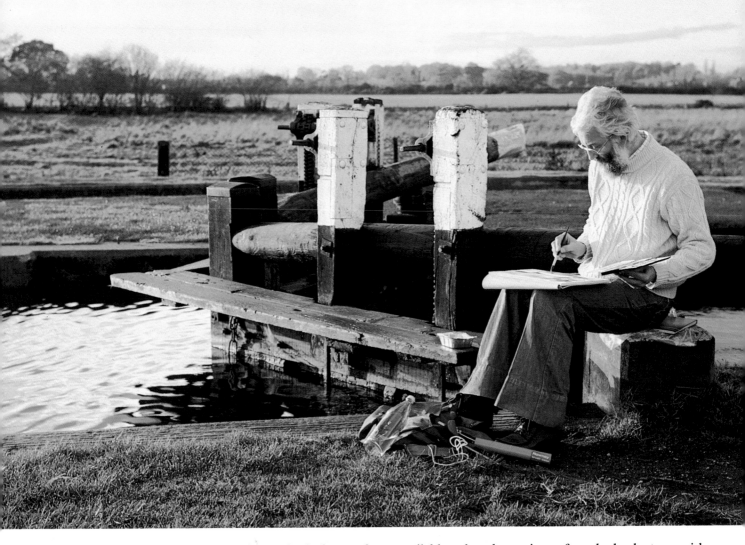

Painting is one of man's earliest and most basic forms of expression. The Stone Age man drew on his cave walls. Usually, these drawings were of wild animals and hunting scenes. It is difficult to say whether these were created by the artist to be instructional – a means of showing his children what a certain animal looked like, for instance – or as a form of cave decoration, or whether they were just a relaxing pastime to release his creative feelings. Whatever the reason, these artists must have been a very creative and dedicated people; there was no local art shop to help them with their materials and no electric light to help on dark days. All this started over twenty-five thousand years ago and painting is still with us today. Naturally, over this long, long period, painting has become very sophisticated. It has survived thousands of years of changing civilisations, styles, ideas and techniques. Artist's materials have also undergone a vast change and the tremendous range now

available, plus the variety of methods that are with us today, can make painting very frightening for the beginner; people can be put off by not knowing where or how to start. One of the most frequent statements made to me is: I wish I could paint. My reply is: Have you tried? and invariably the answer comes: Oh no, I haven't: I wouldn't know where or how to start. How can anyone say they cannot paint when they have never tried? Have you ever asked anyone if they can drive a car? If the answer is no, it will usually be followed by: I failed two tests and gave it up, or: I haven't tried yet but I am going to have lessons. The difference between painting and driving is simple: there seems to be a veil of mystery around painting but not around driving a car. Let me try to clear your mind about some of the mysteries, from a beginner's point of view.

First of all, you may feel daunted by the sheer volume of work that has been created over the past thousands of

Whether you like to paint outside or in your studio, Alwyn Crawshaw will guide you step-by-step as you experiment with styles and techniques of watercolour painting

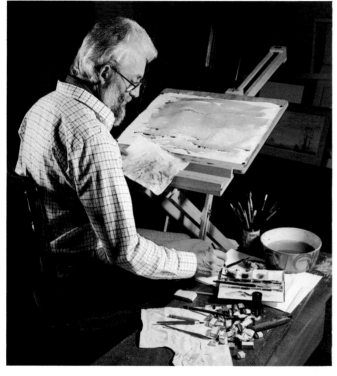

years, the hundreds of styles and techniques used, from painting on ceilings to painting miniatures. Names may confuse you, such as: Prehistoric painting, Greek painting, Egyptian painting, Byzantine painting, Chinese painting, Gothic art, Florentine painting, Impressionism, Surrealism, Abstract art, Cubism, and so on. All these terms make the mind boggle. To unravel all of them and understand the differences could take a lifetime. Then what are we to do and where do we start? The simplest answer is to forget all you have picked up in the past and start from the smallest beginnings, like the Stone Age man.

Today, most people who want to paint have one thing in common – a creative instinct. Unfortunately, some people don't realise this until later on in life when something might stir within them or circumstances set them on the road to painting. For some people painting becomes a fascinating and relaxing hobby. For others it becomes their only way

of expressing their innermost thoughts and leads to a way of communicating with others. For anyone who happens to be house-bound, painting can have a real therapeutic function; through painting, people meet and make friends either by joining art societies (most towns have one) or by progressing and selling their works at local art shows, in local shops and so on. I think, above all, painting can be a creative way of getting involved, forgetting all your immediate troubles, great and small, and finishing up with a work of art that you can share with others and enjoy for the rest of your life.

By now, as the reader of this book, you have taken your first big step: if you are a beginner, this means that you are curious about painting and want to find out all about it. You have also selected a medium with which to start: watercolour. If you already paint and are reading this book to learn about watercolours as another medium, then probably your curiosity and creative instincts are looking for other exciting ways to express your pictorial skills.

Now, as I said a little earlier, let's start right at the beginning. Don't rush out to find the nearest cave! I will take you through this book stage by stage, working very simply to start with and progressing to a more mature form of painting. If you have some watercolours, the most difficult thing to do at the moment will be to read on – your desire to try out the paint will have been stimulated by looking through the book and seeing the colour pages and different methods of working. If this is the case, you are well on your way but do one thing first: relax and read on before you start. When you do start the lessons and exercises – enjoy them. If you find some parts difficult, don't allow yourself to become obsessed with the problem; go a stage further and then come back. Seeing the problem with a fresh eye will make it easier to solve.

WHY USE WATERCOLOURS . . . AND WHAT ARE THEY?

I am constantly asked why I paint in more than one medium. The reasons are varied. An artist sometimes uses a medium because he has been commissioned to do so or because he likes one medium more than another but more important is the fact that each medium has its own mystique and, of course, a particular quality. There is also the restraint of size. For instance, watercolour paper isn't made large enough for a 76 × 152cm (30 × 60in) painting and neither is pastel paper so the medium can determine the size of the painting. Finally, the subject matter has to be considered. When I am out looking for possible subjects I see one as a subject for an acrylic painting, another as a perfect watercolour, and so on.

Whatever *your* reason for choosing watercolour, even if it's the obvious one – you like it! – *you* have made the choice and we will work together over the next fifty-six pages, from simple beginnings to more serious exercises later.

First, a word of caution. Because your earliest recollection of painting – probably when you were at infant school – is associated with the use of water-based paint (poster paint, powder colour or watercolour) you may have the impression that it is easy. Well, of course, to enjoy painting and get favourable results is relatively easy. However, to get the desired results through deliberate *control* of watercolour needs *a lot* of practice and patience but the more you learn, the more you will enjoy using watercolour.

Watercolours are so called because the adhesive that sticks the pigment powder to the paper is soluble in water. The paint is a finely ground mixture of pigment, gum arabic (the water-soluble gum of the acacia tree), glycerine (to keep the colours moist) and glucose (to make the colours flow freely).

When water is loaded on to a brush and added to the paint on the palette, the paint becomes a coloured, transparent liquid. When this is applied to the white surface of the paper, the paper shows through and the paint assumes a transparent luminosity unequalled by any other medium. You buy the colours either in a half pan, a whole pan or a tube (see **fig. 1**). I will explain more about this in the equipment section. One great advantage of watercolour is that it requires no complicated equipment. For painting out-of-doors, for instance, your basic essentials are a box of paints, a brush, paper and water.

You will find that the paint dries within minutes of its application to the paper as the water evaporates, leaving the dry colour on the surface. This process can be seen when working. While the paint is shiny on the paper, it is still

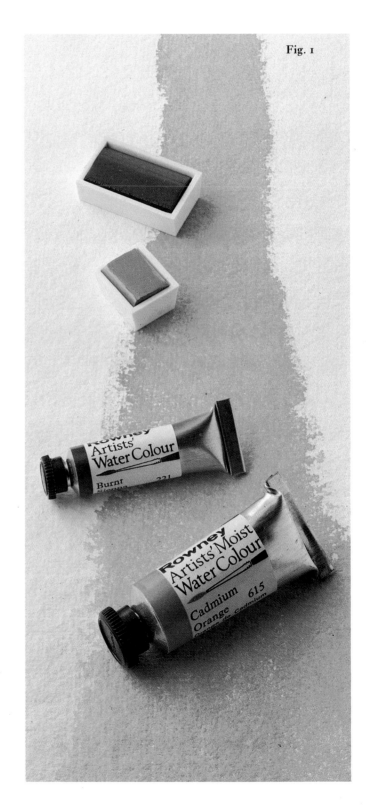

Fig. 1

wet and you can move it about or add more colour with the brush, but as soon as the shine goes off the paper (the paint is now in an advanced drying stage) you must leave it alone and *let it* dry. If you try to work more paint into it, you will get nasty streaks and blotches. Because the paint dries quickly – especially if you are under a hot sun – watercolour painting does not favour faint hearts. If you think you are in that category, don't worry; you will gain confidence as you read and *work* through the book.

Before you start a painting you need to have a plan of campaign in your mind. Naturally, as you progress, this will become second nature to you. When I was at art school I was taught to look and observe and, ever since, I have always looked at the sky as if it were a painting and considered how it had been done – in which medium, with which brush, which colour was used first, and so on. I see things as shapes and colours, and techniques of painting. The strange thing is that I see most things as watercolour paintings. I think this is because of the very nature of the medium: you have limited time, you are painting from light to dark (more about that later), a bad mistake can't be overpainted (in true watercolour) and, therefore, it all comes down to observation and planning. Nevertheless, you will have to accept the fact that not every watercolour painting is a success – *not to you*, the artist, that is. You will find that you paint a beautiful picture, everyone likes it and it is worthy of being put into an exhibition, but there will be passages of that painting where the watercolour was not completely under your control and it made up its own mind about the final effect. Well, this is an accepted characteristic of *watercolour* painting – only the artist knows how he made the paint behave or misbehave. But when you paint a good picture with plenty of watercolour effect and it was *all* under your control, then you will have achieved a small, personal ambition which will no doubt elevate you into that special band of dedicated watercolourists.

Opposite is a list of the available colours. The colours illustrated are those that I use, set out in my palette order, and will be referred to throughout this book. This colour chart is produced within the limitations of printing and is intended as a guide only.

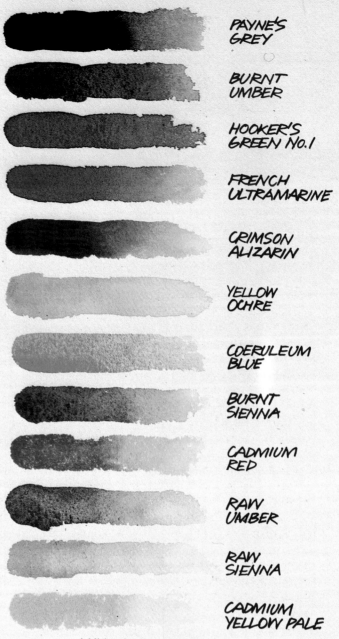

PAYNE'S GREY

BURNT UMBER

HOOKER'S GREEN No. 1

FRENCH ULTRAMARINE

CRIMSON ALIZARIN

YELLOW OCHRE

COERULEUM BLUE

BURNT SIENNA

CADMIUM RED

RAW UMBER

RAW SIENNA

CADMIUM YELLOW PALE

Additional colours available

Chinese White	Indigo
Chrome Lemon	Monestial Blue
Chrome Orange	Permanent Red
Chrome Orange Deep	Permanent Sepia
Chrome Yellow	Permanent Yellow
Hooker's Green No 2	Purple Lake
Indian Red	Purple Madder (Alizarin)
Ivory Black	Rose Dore (Alizarin)
Lamp Black	Scarlet Alizarin
Light Red	Scarlet Lake
Naples Yellow	Violet Alizarin
Olive Green	Aureolin
Permanent Blue	Cobalt Blue
Permanent Magenta	Cobalt Green
Permanent Mauve	Cobalt Violet
Prussian Blue	Gamboge (Hue)
Sap Green	Lemon Yellow
Terre Verte	Viridian
Vandyke Brown	Cadmium Orange
Venetian Red	Cadmium Yellow
Alizarin Green	Cadmium Yellow Deep
Brown Madder (Alizarin)	Permanent Rose
Brown Pink	Carmine
Crimson Lake	Scarlet Vermilion
Indian Yellow	

WHAT EQUIPMENT DO YOU NEED?

Every professional artist has his favourite brushes, colours, and so on. In the end, the choice must be left to you, to make from your personal experience.

In the last chapter I gave you a list of the colours that I use. I suggest that you, too, use these as you work through this book because I shall refer to them to describe different colour mixes. You may find that you prefer to drop a couple of colours or change some once you have made some progress – this will be fine and, of course, it also applies to other materials used in the exercises.

To get the best results, you should use the best materials you can afford. The two main distinctions between different watercolour paints are cost and quality. The best quality watercolours are called *Artists' Quality Water Colours* and those a grade lower are called *students' water colours*, some of which are manufactured under brand names such as *Georgian Water Colours*. Watercolour paints can be bought in a water colour box, empty or ready filled with colours (see **fig. 2**), or in separate pans which you can use as refills or to fill an empty box with your own choice of colours. **Fig. 2** shows one box of half pans, one of whole pans and a very small box that contains eighteen quarter-pans of colour, measures only 13 × 5cm (5 × 2in) and has a leatherette case. This last box is ideal for keeping in your pocket or handbag to use for impromptu sketching. The last two boxes illustrated carry tubes of paint – you have to squeeze the colour on to the palette (the open lid of the box) and use the paint as if you were working from pans. Colours in tubes are ideal for quickly saturating a brush in strong colour, using less water, but I do not advise beginners to use tubes because it is difficult to control the amount of paint on the brush. You can buy additional palettes for mixing your colours and you can see these on page 13 in the illustration of my studio working area. This has been over-crowded intentionally, to accommodate all the different materials you might require as you progress. At the end of this chapter is a list of basic, beginner's equipment.

Now we come to the tools of the trade – brushes. The best quality, watercolour brushes are made from kolinsky sable. They are hand made and are the most expensive brushes on the market but they give you perfect control over your brush strokes and, if properly cared for, will last a long time. Also in the fine-quality range of watercolour brushes, but less expensive, are those made with squirrel hair, ox-ear hair and ringcat hair. Man-made fibres are also used in the manufacture of artists' brushes and an excellent range of white nylon brushes became available in the mid-1970s. Remember, brushes are the tools with which you express yourself on paper. It is only your use of the brush that reveals your skill to the onlooker and this applies to watercolour more than any other medium. *One brush stroke* can express a field, a lake, the side of a boat, and

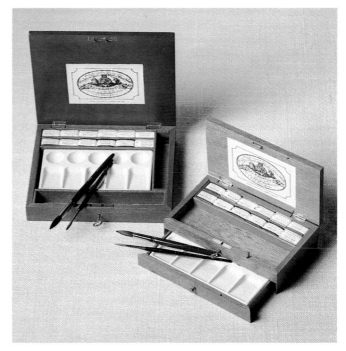

Both these boxes are copies of original Artists' Water Colour Boxes first sold by Thomas and Richard Rowney between 1795 and 1810

so on; therefore, you must know your brushes and what to expect from them. There are two basic types: a round brush and a flat brush. If you look at **fig. 3** you will see brushes of different shapes, made from different hairs. Usually, the handles of watercolour brushes are short but where the brush can also be used for oil or acrylic painting, the handle may be longer – the flat, ox-ear-hair brush, Series 62, is a good example. The round brush is a general purpose one: both a wash and a thin line can be obtained with this shape. The flat brush is used mainly for putting washes over large areas or where a broad brush stroke is called for. Naturally, the width of these strokes is determined by the size of the flat brush. Usually, round brushes are graded from size No. 00 to size No. 12 and some manufacturers make a No. 14 size. This scale can be seen in **fig. 3** and the brushes are reproduced actual size. Flat brushes and very large brushes, such as the squirrel-hair wash brush, have a name or size of their own.

Watercolour paper, of course, is a very important piece of equipment – so important, in fact, that I have put it in a section of its own on pages 14 and 15.

Other items you need are pencils – start by getting an HB and 2B (the other grades up to 6B, the softest, I will leave to your own choice); a good quality, natural sponge for wetting the paper or sponging off areas you want to repaint; blotting paper for absorbing wet colour from the

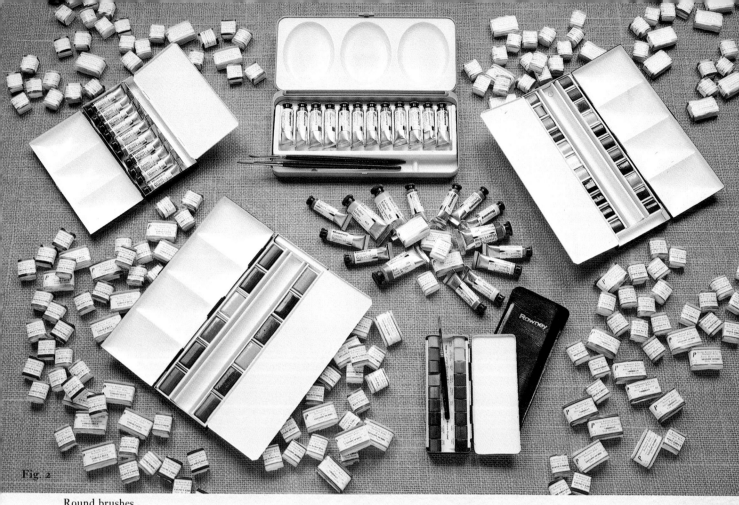

Fig. 2

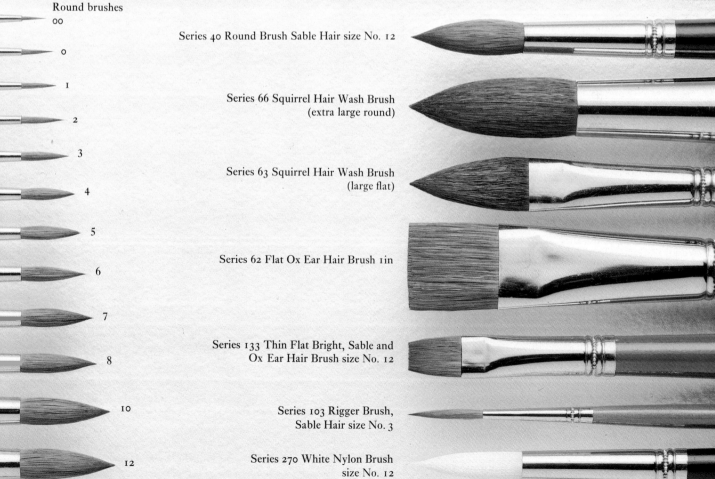

Round brushes

00

0

1

2

3

4

5

6

7

8

10

12

Series 40 Round Brush Sable Hair size No. 12

Series 66 Squirrel Hair Wash Brush
(extra large round)

Series 63 Squirrel Hair Wash Brush
(large flat)

Series 62 Flat Ox Ear Hair Brush 1in

Series 133 Thin Flat Bright, Sable and
Ox Ear Hair Brush size No. 12

Series 103 Rigger Brush,
Sable Hair size No. 3

Series 270 White Nylon Brush
size No. 12

Fig. 3   All brushes are shown actual size. Some brush series have additional sizes to those shown, i.e. 9, 11 and 14

surface of the paper in order to lighten a passage that is too dark; and a brush case, very necessary when you are painting outside (see **fig. 4**) to avoid damaging your brushes.

You need a drawing board on which to pin your paper. You can make one from a smooth piece of plywood or you can buy one from your local art shop. A container to hold your painting water can be anything from a jam jar to a plastic cup but make sure that it is big enough to hold plenty of water, and *keep changing* the water so that it is always clean. A kneadable putty rubber is the best type to use for erasing as it can be used gently on delicate paper without causing too much damage to the surface. When you are using a pen and wash technique in the exercises, you will require a mapping pen and black Indian ink.

A watercolour is never painted right up to the edge of the paper so it is a good idea to have some mounts for offering up to a finished watercolour. You will then be able to see where the painting will be masked when it is framed. Cut mounts of various sizes from cartridge paper or thin card and when you have finished a painting, put a mount around it to see what you think. This will help you decide whether you think your picture looks finished or not.

Now for your essential equipment: you will see what you need in **fig. 5**. You can start with only three brushes: a size No. 10 round brush (the quality you get will depend on the price), a size No. 6 round brush for general detail work and either a squirrel-hair wash brush or a one-inch, flat, ox-ear-hair brush for covering extra-large areas with washes. You need a paint box to hold 12 colours in half pans or whole pans, HB and 2B pencils, a kneadable putty rubber, a drawing board, paper, blotting paper, a sponge and a water jar. I haven't included an easel because it is not an essential piece of watercolour equipment; when you are working outside, your painting is usually small enough to manage on a drawing board or watercolour block (see page 14) resting on your knees.

This short list represents the advantages of watercolour: its equipment, its approach and its execution are simple. However, although you can have a lot of fun with it, you can achieve complete control over watercolour only after a great deal of experience.

Back to the drawing board – or easel. You can work very comfortably at a table, with the top edge of your drawing board supported by a book or piece of wood about 8–10cm (3–4in) high so that the washes can run down correctly. If you want to work on an easel, choose one from the variety on the market.

Fig. 4 Brush case

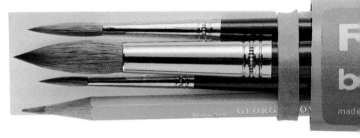

Fig. 5 Beginner's basic equipment

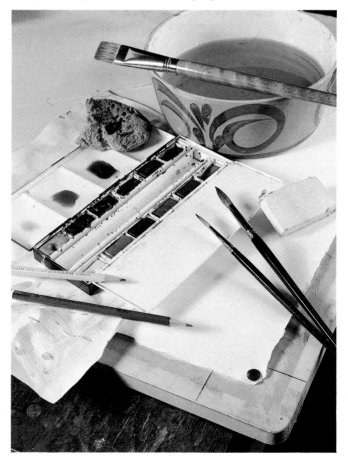

A STRETCHED PAPER
B VARIOUS BRUSHES & PENCILS
C MIXING PALETTES
D WATER CONTAINER
E SPONGE
F WATER COLOUR BOX WITH TUBES
G WATER COLOUR BOX WITH WHOLE PANS
H BLACK INK
I PUTTY RUBBER
J PENCILS & MAPPING PENS
K TUBES, WHOLE PANS & HALF PANS
L MIXING PALETTES
M POCKET SIZE WATER COLOUR BOX (5"x2")
N VARIOUS BRUSHES WITH BRUSH CASE
O CARD MOUNTS
P OUTDOOR STOOL
Q STUDIO EASEL
R BLOTTING PAPER
S WATER COLOUR BLOCK
T VARIOUS PAPERS ON DRAWING BOARD

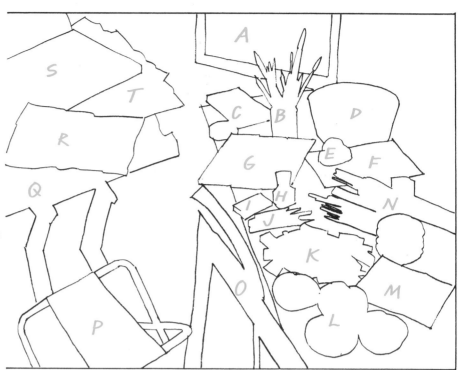

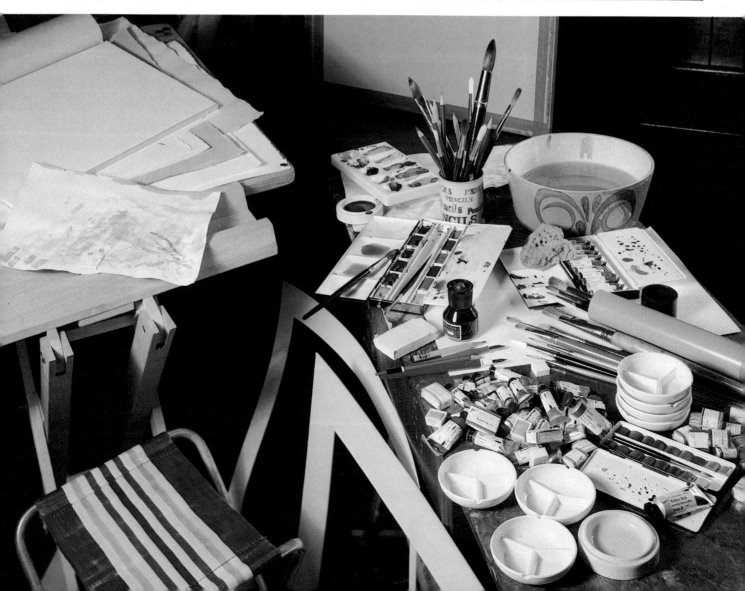

WHICH PAPER?

You can paint with watercolour on almost any type of paper. You can work on drawing paper, on the inside of a cardboard carton, or even on the back of a roll of wallpaper. Naturally, there are problems in using any old paper. Firstly, if the paper is too absorbent, the liquid will be sucked into the surface like ink on blotting paper and secondly, if the surface is non-absorbent, the paint will run completely out of control. The answer, then, is to use paper that has been specially made for the watercolour artist. The finest quality papers are made by hand, by craftsmen whose skills have been handed down over the centuries. Up to the beginning of the nineteenth century, even the cheapest wrapping paper was made by hand but then, machinery took over a great proportion of the production. Because the best quality, watercolour paper is still made by hand it is very expensive. However, in comparison with a ready-stretched canvas of equivalent size, top-quality paper is far cheaper – and each of them produces only one picture.

Watercolour papers have a unique, surface texture that is sympathetic to the brush – artists usually refer to it as a tooth. It is this tooth that responds to the brush and helps create the unique, watercolour effect. The paper also has just the right amount of absorbency to hold the liquid colour under manageable control. There are many types of paper on the market but they all have two things in common: they are all finished with one of three kinds of surface texture and they are all graded by weight (this tells us the thickness of the paper). The surfaces are: *Rough*, *Not* (the Americans call this *Cold Pressed*) and *Hot Pressed* (HP). Paper with a Rough surface has a very pronounced texture (tooth) and is usually used for large paintings where bold, vigorous brush work is required. The Not surface has less tooth and this is the one most commonly used by artists; it is also ideal for the beginner. The Hot Pressed surface is very smooth, with very little tooth, and before you try this paper you need to know how to handle your watercolour: if you use the paint very wet, it can easily run, concerned only for its own destination and your downfall!

Usually, you buy watercolour paper in an Imperial size (approximately 31 × 22in) but hand-made paper sizes can vary by a few inches.

The weight of the paper is arrived at by calculating how much a ream (480 sheets) weighs. For instance, if a ream weighs 300lb (which is about the heaviest paper you can use) then the paper is called (with its manufacturer's name and surface title) *Greens Pasteless Board 300lb Not*. You will find that a good weight to work on is a 140lb paper. If this sounds complicated, don't worry. To start with, get used to two or three types of paper. You will learn how the paper reacts to the paint and what you can and can't do. This is as important as getting used to your brushes and colours. When you first buy paper, pencil the name, size and weight in each corner for future reference. On the opposite page are pieces of watercolour paper, reproduced their actual size. I have put some paint on each one and I have also given its full description.

Paper tends to cockle when you put wet paint on it and the thinner the paper the more it will cockle. I have explained below how to get over this problem by stretching the paper. (Heavy and thick papers do not need stretching.) Paper can also be bought in sheets stuck together on the edges of all four sides to prevent cockling. These are called water colour blocks, they come in various sizes and are excellent for use out-of-doors. When the painting is finished, you simply tear off the sheet and work on the next one.

When you have practised and have become confident in handling your colours without spoiling too much paper, buy the best paper you can afford and stick to that one until you know it like the back of your hand. The better you know your brushes, your paints *and* your paper, the more you will enjoy painting – and the better your results will be.

How to stretch your paper

Cut a sheet of paper the size you need but *smaller* than your drawing board, submerge it in a sink full of water or hold it under a running tap and *completely soak* both sides. Hold it up by one end, let the surface water drain off, then lay it on a *wooden* drawing board. Use a roll of brown, gummed paper to stick the four sides down, allowing the gummed paper to fall half over the paper and half over the board. Now leave it to dry naturally, overnight. In the morning, it will be as tight as a drum and as flat as a pancake, and it will stay flat while you work. The finished result is shown in the photograph at the top of the page. It is heaven to work on.

GREENS PASTELESS BOARD 300lb Rough

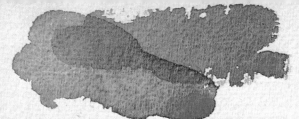

FABRIANO CLASSICO 5 281lb Rough

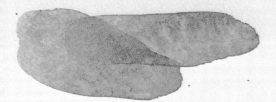

GREENS PASTELESS BOARD 300lb HP

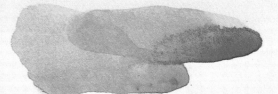

FABRIANO CLASSICO 5 140lb HP

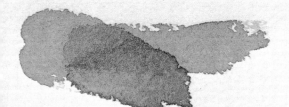

GREENS PASTELESS BOARD 300lb Not

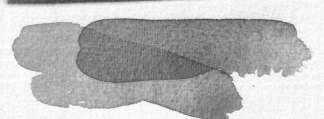

FABRIANO CLASSICO 5 281lb Not

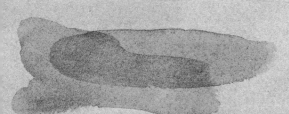

GREENS TURNER GREY 72lb Not

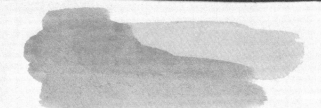

'GEORGIAN' WATER COLOUR PAPER 140lb

GREENS DE WINT 90lb Rugged

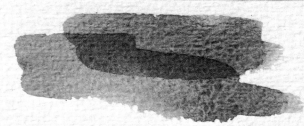

ARTISTS SUPERIOR QUALITY BOCKINGFORD
WATER COLOUR PAPER 300 gm²

GREENS CAMBER SAND 72lb Not

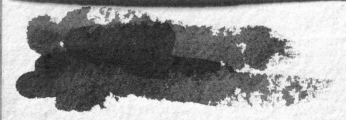

GREENS R.W.S. 140lb Rough

LET'S START PAINTING

PLAYING WITH PAINT

At last, you can start painting. A lot of people who have not painted before find this the most difficult bridge to cross – to actually put some paint on paper. Unfortunately, we are all self-conscious when doing things we have never tried before and our families don't help either! I have often come across the case of a member of the family who sees someone's first efforts at painting. Remarks such as What's that! and Oh well, never mind, are never meant to hurt or be unkind, but, unfortunately, they can put off a sensitive beginner – sometimes for ever. Well, this is how we will get over that problem, if it arises. It's human nature for us all to strive to do better and if we try to run before we can walk, then this is when disaster will strike and cause those humorous comments from the rest of the family. So we will start at the very beginning and take things in a steady, progressive order – I'll see you don't run first.

Let us take colours as our first step. A beginner may find the hundreds of colours that exist somewhat overwhelming. But the choice can be simplified: there are only three basic colours, *red*, *yellow* and *blue* which are called primary colours (see the illustration opposite) and all other colours, and shades of colour, are formed by a combination of these three. In painting, there are different reds, yellows and blues which we can use to help recreate nature's colours. Look at the illustration again and you will see that there are two of each primary colour. As I have explained earlier, these colours, plus another six, are the ones I use, for all my watercolour painting.

Before you start mixing colours, get yourself a piece of watercolour paper or cartridge paper and *play* with the paint on this. See what it feels like, try different brushes, add more water, less water, mix colours together. You will end up with a funny-looking, coloured piece of paper. Incidentally, if the family laugh at this one, laugh with them, show them my doodles on paper and laugh at that! What you have done is to experience the feel of watercolour paint. You will have noticed that if you add more water, you make the colour lighter. This is the correct method for making watercolours lighter, not by adding white paint. The paint isn't a stranger to you any more, nor are your brushes or paper. You have now broken the ice and will feel much more confident in tackling the next section. Good luck.

MIXING COLOURS

As we progress through the exercises, I will help you as much as I can but you must first spend some time practising mixing different colours. Look at the illustration opposite. I have taken the primary colours and mixed them to show you the results. In the first row, Cadmium Yellow Pale mixed with French Ultramarine makes green. In the second row, Cadmium Yellow Pale mixed with Cadmium Red makes orange. To make the orange look more yellow, add more yellow than red and to make it more red, add more red than yellow. Add more water to make the orange paler.

You may have noticed that my colours do not include black. Some artists use black and other's don't. I am one of the don'ts. I don't use black because I believe it is a dead colour, too flat. Therefore, I mix my blacks from the primary colours and I suggest that you do the same. Remember that, in general, if you want a colour to be cooler, add blue and if it is to be warmer, then add red.

Practise mixing different colours on white cartridge paper. Mix the colours on your palette with a brush and paint daubs on to your white paper. Don't worry about shapes at this stage, it's the colours you're trying for. Experiment and practise – that is the only real advice I can give you, here. When you're next sitting down, look around you, pick a colour that you can see and try to imagine what colours you would use to mix it.

One last, important point: when there are only three basic colours it is the *amount* of each colour that plays the biggest part. You can easily mix a green as in the second line opposite, but if it is to be a yellowy green, you have to experiment on your palette; you have to mix and work in more yellow until you have the colour you want. This lesson of mixing colours is one that you will be practising and improving upon all your life – I am, still.

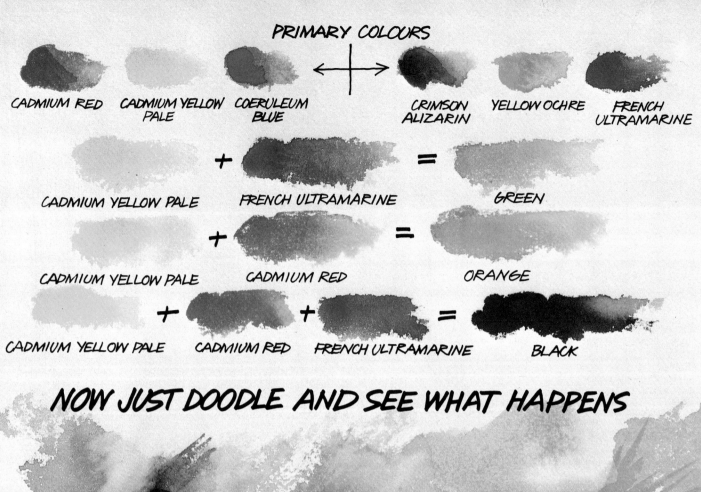

PRIMARY COLOURS

CADMIUM RED CADMIUM YELLOW PALE COERULEUM BLUE CRIMSON ALIZARIN YELLOW OCHRE FRENCH ULTRAMARINE

CADMIUM YELLOW PALE + FRENCH ULTRAMARINE = GREEN

CADMIUM YELLOW PALE + CADMIUM RED = ORANGE

CADMIUM YELLOW PALE + CADMIUM RED + FRENCH ULTRAMARINE = BLACK

NOW JUST DOODLE AND SEE WHAT HAPPENS

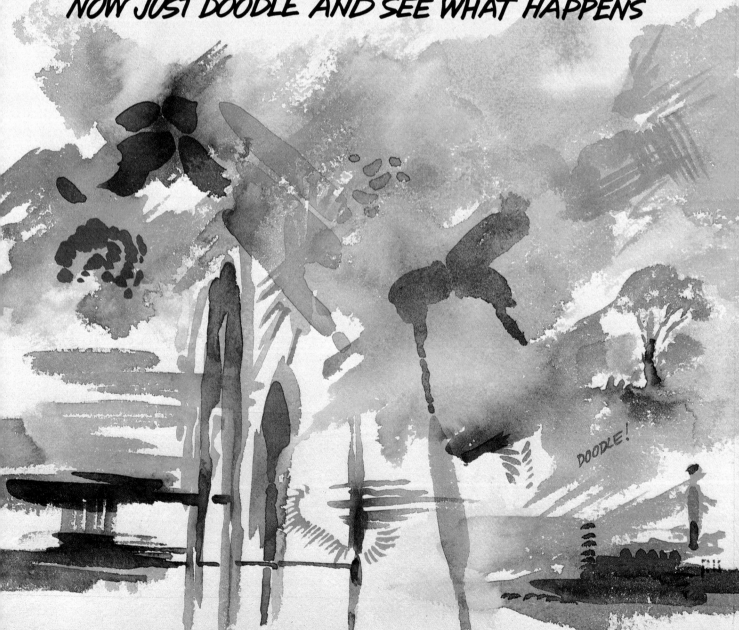

DOODLE!

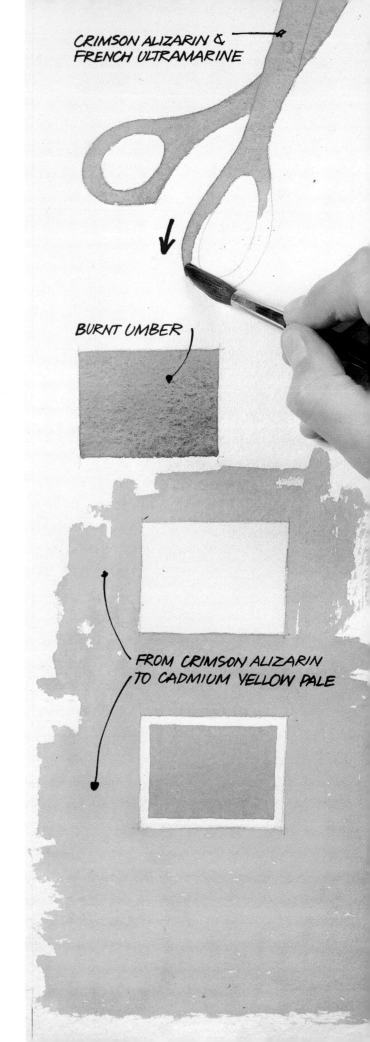

Fig. 6

BRUSH CONTROL

Now you must learn to control the paint brush. Like all things, when you know how, it is much easier than you had thought. A lot of control is required when painting edges of areas that have to be filled in with paint, such as the outline of a pair of scissors (**fig. 6**).

Take a pair of scissors, or anything handy that has round shapes, and draw round it with an HB pencil. You can do this on cartridge paper or watercolour paper. Use your round sable brush with plenty of water. When you start to fill in the curved shapes, start at the top and work down the left side, to the bottom (**fig. 6**). Let the bristles follow the brush, i.e. pull the brush down. Try to do this in two or three movements. When you paint the right side of the handle, your brush will cover some of the pencil lines and you will feel slightly awkward. The answer is to accept that it feels a bit awkward but the more you use your brush like that, the more natural it will feel – practise!

Now, let's go on to straight lines. This time, draw a square, like the side of a box. Try this one freehand, don't draw around anything. Here is a *very important* rule to remember: when you draw straight lines (unless you are drawing very short ones), always move your wrist and arm – not your fingers. Try this with a pencil – first, draw a straight line downwards, moving only your fingers. You will find that you can draw only a few centimetres before your fingers make the line bend. Now do the same exercise but keep your fingers firm and move only your hand, bending your arm at the elbow. The result will be a long, straight line.

You can paint the edges of the box with the round sable brush again. Use this same brush for filling in the square with the rest of the paint (see **fig. 7**).

Draw another two squares like the one in **fig. 7** and paint both up to the outside edges. Then, paint another box inside the bottom box, without drawing it first. Also, change the colour as you paint, working from the top box to the bottom one. This one will keep you busy!

Now draw your own shapes and fill them in, mixing your own colours. Look around and choose a colour, perhaps the colour of your carpet or a cushion, then try to mix a colour like it to use for painting in your shapes. You are practising all you have learned so far, in one exercise: well done – but keep at it, enjoy it and keep practising.

CRIMSON ALIZARIN & FRENCH ULTRAMARINE

BURNT UMBER

FROM CRIMSON ALIZARIN TO CADMIUM YELLOW PALE

Fig. 7

SIMPLE PERSPECTIVE AND DRAWING

Drawing, or the knowledge of drawing, comes before painting and, therefore, we will take a little time to practise simple perspective. If you believe you can't draw, don't let this worry you. Some artists can paint a picture but would have difficulty in drawing it as a drawing in its own right. It is the colours, the tones and the shapes of the masses that make a painting.

Over the centuries, artists have always invented and used drawing aids. Today, there is a very simple, but very effective, aid to drawing on the market, called a *Perspectograph* – it sorts out the perspective for you. But it is not too difficult to do this yourself.

When you look out to sea, the horizon will always be at your eye level, even if you climb a cliff or lie flat on the sand. So the horizon is the eye level (E.L.). If you are in a room, naturally, there is no horizon but you still have an eye level. To find this, hold your pencil horizontally in front of your eyes at arm's length: your eye level is where the pencil hits the opposite wall. If two parallel lines were marked out on the ground and extended to the horizon, they would come together at what is called the vanishing point. This is why railway lines appear to get closer together and finally meet in the distance – they have met at the vanishing point (V.P.).

First, look at **fig. 8A**. I have taken our box, the square you drew in the previous section, and put it on paper. Then I drew a line above to represent the eye level. Then, to the right-hand end of the E.L., I made a mark, the V.P. With a ruler I drew a line from each of the four corners of the box, all converging at the V.P. This gave me the two sides, the bottom and the top of the box. To create the other end of the box, I drew a square parallel with the front of the box and kept it within the V.P. guide lines. The effect is that of a transparent box drawn in perspective. Incidentally, we are looking down on this box because the eye level is high. In **fig. 8B** I have shaded the box with pencil to show the light direction.

Figs. 8C, D and **E** show the same box, the first one painted all over with a wash of Hooker's Green No. 1; the second box painted with a second wash over two sides when the first wash had dried; the third one painted with an additional wash on the darkest side, which made the box appear solid. The last one (**fig. 8F**) shows the same drawing painted to represent a hollow box.

This is a simple exercise but it is the most important exercise you will ever do. You are creating on a flat surface the illusion of depth, dimension and perspective; in other words, a three-dimensional object.

Fig. 8

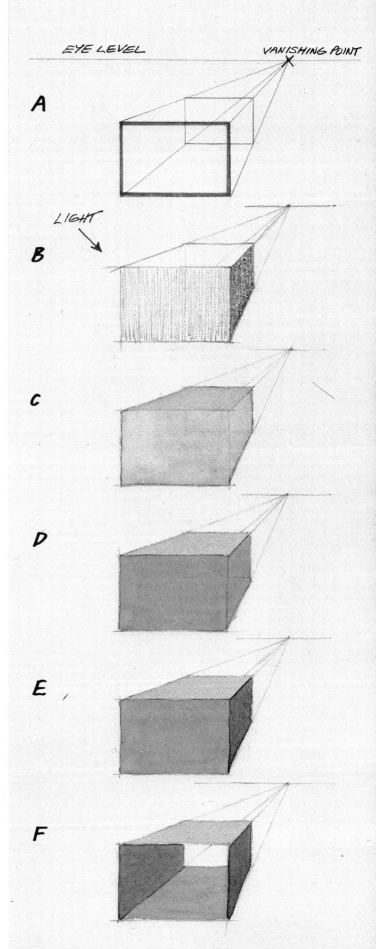

EYE LEVEL   VANISHING POINT

A

LIGHT

B

C

D

E

F

BASIC WATERCOLOUR TECHNIQUES

Before you start these basic techniques, read the next three paragraphs carefully.

When you put the first wash on the box (**fig. 8C**) did you notice that, although the box was drawn in perspective, it looked flat? This is because there was no light or shade (light against dark). It is this light against dark that enables us to see objects and understand their form. If we were to paint our box red, on a background coloured the same red, without adding light or shade (light against dark) we would not be able to see it. If light and shade were added, it could then be seen. You must always be conscious of light against dark whenever you are painting. When you are painting a still life or outside, it will help you to see shapes if you look at the scene through half-closed eyes. The lights and darks will be exaggerated and the middle tones will tend to disappear: this will enable you to see simple, contrasting shapes to follow.

You will see that while your colour is wet, it appears dark and rich but when it is dry, it is slightly lighter. You will learn from experience how to adjust the density of your colours in order to achieve the desired effect. In the meantime, don't worry – it won't spoil your paintings. Don't get too depressed if you feel a painting has gone wrong or out of control. It happens to the best of watercolour artists – it's

part of watercolour painting. Remember: you can learn a lot from your mistakes.

When using colours, you must always work to one *very* important rule: your colours must always be in the same position in your paint box and you must always use the box the same way round. You will have enough to think about, without wondering where your colours are, when you are in the middle of painting a wash. The position of the colours in my box is shown on page 12 and I have my box with the deep wash pans (in the lid) on the left of the box. I was taught to work this way at art school and I have done so ever since.

Now, we can study the most basic technique of watercolour painting – *the flat wash*.

In all instructive illustrations I have used arrows to help you understand the movement of the brush. The solid-black arrow shows the direction of the brush stroke and the outline arrow shows the direction in which the brush is travelling over the paper. For example, **fig. 9** shows the brush stroke moving horizontally, from left to right, and the brush moving down the paper after the completion of each horizontal stroke.

For a flat wash you need *plenty* of watery paint in your palette. *Load* your largest brush and start at the top, left-

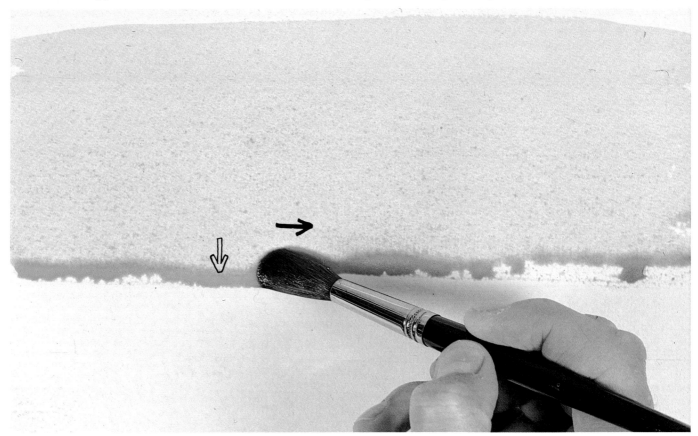

Fig. 9

Fig. 11

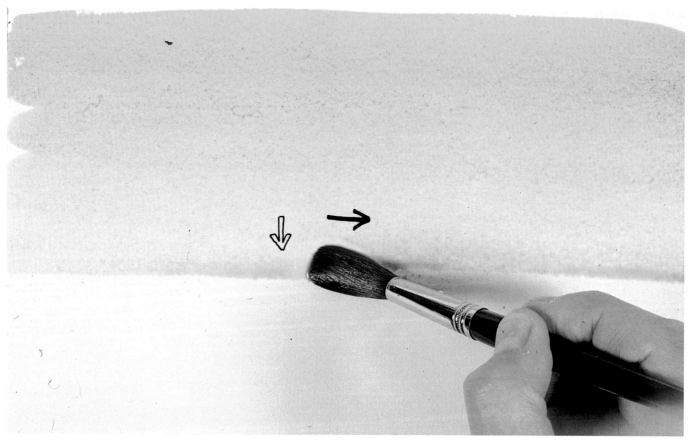

hand side of the paper, taking the brush along in a definite movement. Don't rush. When you get to the end, bring the brush back, run it slightly into the first wet stroke and make another brush stroke like the first. You will, of course, add more paint to your brush when you need it. Because the colour was mixed before you started the wash and you have added no more water, the colour density of the wash should be the same all the way down. Let this wash dry, then paint another one over it, using the same colour but leaving about one centimetre (half an inch) at the top of the original wash. If you repeat this process at least six times, you will begin to get the knack of putting on a wash, you will practise the watercolour technique of applying transparent colour over and over again, and you will see that the more washes you apply, the darker the colour becomes (see **fig. 10**).

Graded wash

A graded wash is produced in exactly the same way as a flat wash except that, as you travel down the paper, you add more *clean* water to the colour in your palette. This weakens the density of the colour, with the result that the wash gets progressively paler from top to bottom (see **fig. 11**).

Fig. 10

Fig. 12

Wet on wet

The term wet on wet is common to all painting mediums and means that wet paint is applied over existing wet paint. It is one of the most intriguing, watercolour techniques. It is impossible to predict exactly what will happen when you put wet paint on top of a wet wash (see **figs. 12** and **13**). This is precisely why it is such a fascinating technique. You will create some fantastic effects – some of them dramatic, others subtle.

You can see one of my experiments in **fig. 12**. I painted Coeruleum Blue first, very wet. Then, I added a mix of Payne's Grey and Burnt Umber, very wet, in the middle. When this was dry, I lightly sponged it with clean water, then attacked the middle again with a mix of Payne's Grey, French Ultramarine and Burnt Umber – this is very strong colour. Immediately, I added more water to the mix and put a daub on each side of the centre.

If you wait until the first wash is drying, you will have more control over the paint and you will also achieve a slightly different effect. You can get good skies, using the wet on wet technique, by sponging your paper first with clean water, then painting your sky colours and letting them run together.

You need to experiment with this technique and practise control. The overall effect is planned – it's the unpredictable wanderings of the paint that add interest and beauty. When it is dry you might see an area that, by happy accident, needs only a brush stroke to make it read better: if the brush stroke is applied correctly, this passage could be a little gem in the painting.

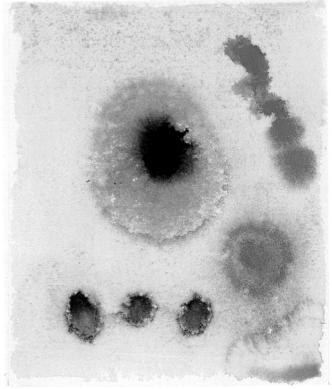

Fig. 13

Fig. 15

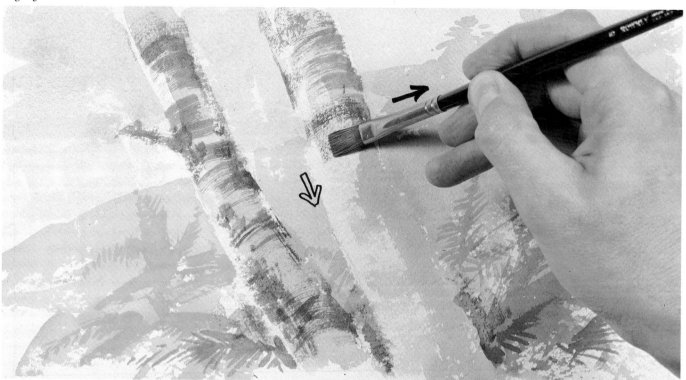

Fig. 14

Dry brush

Dry brush is another technique that is used in most types of painting. It simply means that a brush is damp-dried before being dipped into the paint or else a wet brush is loaded with paint, dried out to a damp consistency on a piece of blotting paper and then applied to the watercolour paper. The technique is used to achieve a hit-and-miss effect. If you try this on rough watercolour paper, it is relatively easy but on a smooth-surfaced paper it needs a little more practise. The chances are that you accidentally produced a dry brush effect when you were doodling or painting the boxes earlier on – you were probably annoyed because you were running out of paint – but it was unintentional and, therefore, uncontrolled.

The best way to get used to the dry brush technique is to use long brush strokes, from left to right, with only a little paint (see **fig. 14**). You will find that your brush runs out of wet paint and finishes the stroke with a dry brush effect. Try to control the amount of wet paint you load on to your brush and take it over, say 30cm so that the stroke is finished with a dry brush. When you can do this, you have gone a long way towards controlling your watercolour brush-work. In **fig. 15** I used a size No. 6 Series 220 nylon brush for the dry brush strokes.

DIFFERENT WAYS TO PAINT

Watercolour is a very versatile medium. It can be used in different ways by different artists. For instance, six artists could paint the same subject, using the same technique, but each painting would be different. In other words, each artist would have his own style. But my wet on wet watercolour, opposite, is painted in a completely different style to my pen and wash watercolour on page 27. Therefore, an artist's style is, to some extent, altered by the technique. To avoid confusion, in this chapter the word style refers to the individual artist's way of painting and the word technique refers to the method of using the paint.

On the following pages are six pictures I have painted of the same subject, using a different technique each time, to show you the versatility and beauty of watercolour. My purpose is to enable you to compare several versions of the *same subject* so that you can see the difference between each technique. The actual size of each painting is 34.4 × 23cm

(13½ × 9in) and the type of paper I used is indicated below each one.

I must point out that some subjects do not necessarily lend themselves to a particular technique and, on the other hand, some subjects cry out for just one technique. Therefore, you must choose your subject and technique carefully. Naturally, a pencil-and-wash or pen-and-wash drawing can be tackled only if you have a reasonable knowledge of drawing because this plays a large part in these two watercolour techniques.

Whatever the technique, the basis for the painting is still the wash – whether it be flat, graded or wet on wet. I mention this at this stage because you just can't practise them enough – the wash *is* watercolour. When you can master it on all scales, small and large, you will be much more relaxed when you work and you will find that fewer disasters come off the brush. Keep practising.

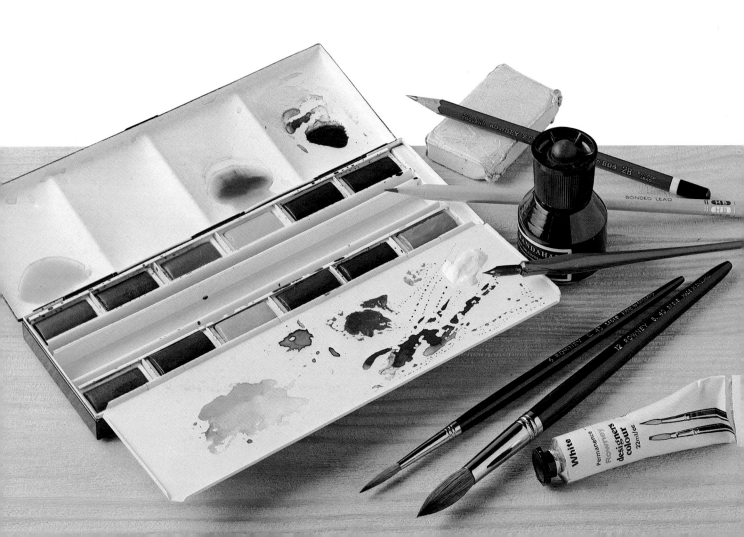

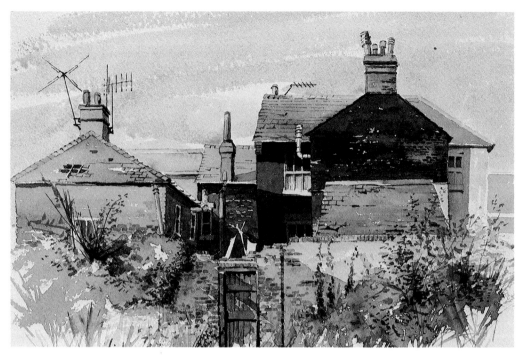

Flat wash and graded wash   Greens Pasteless Board 300lb Not

Flat wash and graded wash

I regard the flat wash and graded wash as basic, traditional ways of using watercolour. Having thought out the moves very carefully beforehand, you work up the effect with washes. Remember to use the lightest colours first and work gradually to the darker tones.

Here, I feel I must make an observation about the buildings. It has always been thought that something old – especially a building – has plenty of character and is a perfect subject for the painter. I agree with this. When television boomed in the 1960s, artists avoided the old buildings that had TV aerials fixed to them, or just left the aerials out. The strange thing is that, when I found the

buildings for the pictures on the following pages, I felt that the TV aerials *added to their character and charm*. It is amazing how things gradually become accepted.

Wet on wet

The wet on wet technique is a very exciting way of using watercolour but it can be also very nerve-racking. The freedom, the apparent ease and the sheer audacity of letting colours make their own way around the paper excites artist and onlooker alike. But although the finished result looks natural and unlaboured, you have to put in many hours of patient practice. Both these paintings were done on Greens Pasteless Board 300lb Not.

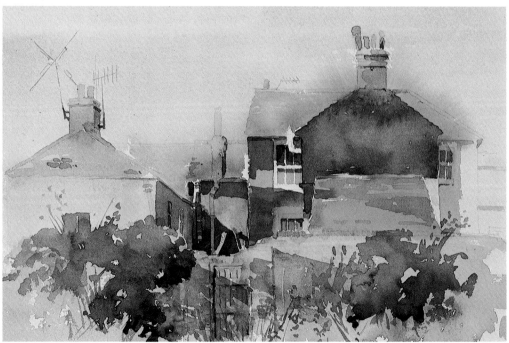

Wet on wet   Greens Pasteless Board 300lb Not

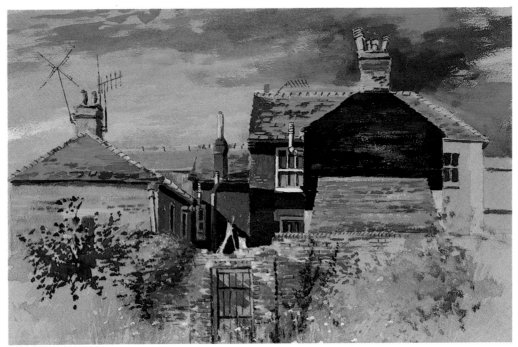

Body colour   Greens Turner Grey 72lb Not

Body colour

You can strengthen your colours by using the body colour technique. Simply add White to the paint and this will immediately take away the transparency of the colour. Generally speaking, instead of water, White is used in this technique to make the colours lighter.

I painted the picture, above, on a Greens Turner Grey 72lb Not paper. I made the sky dark for a dramatic effect and I used pure White where the sun catches the window frame. When you are next painting a watercolour, if you find you have lost it, try using White with your colours and turn it into a body colour painting. Remember that light can be added over dark.

Open wash

This painting looks a little flat when compared with the others but it demonstrates a crisp, clean watercolour technique. I have called the technique open wash because white paper is left between each wash. Apart from its own charm, open wash has a very valuable application. When you are painting outside, it is often impractical to wait for each wash to dry before applying the adjacent one. If you use this method, you can carry on almost without stopping.

The paper I used for this painting, below, is Fabriano Classico 5 28lb Not.

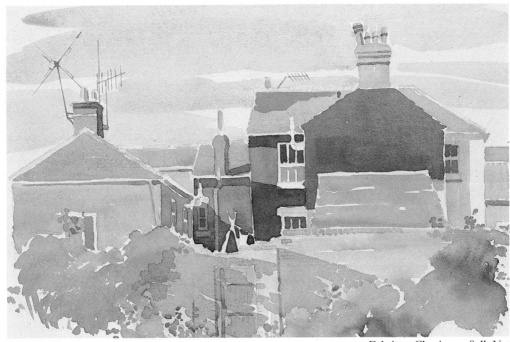

Open wash   Fabriano Classico 5 28lb Not

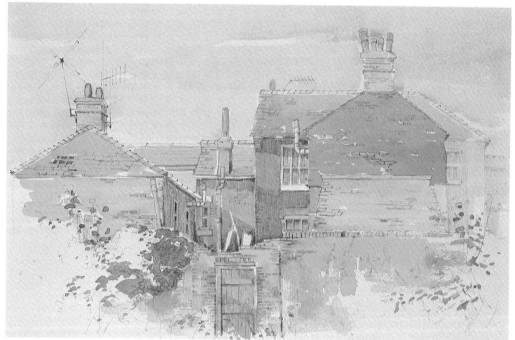

Pencil and wash

Greens Camber Sand 72lb Not

Pencil and wash

I used Greens Camber Sand 72lb Not paper for this paint-ing, above. Pencil and wash is one of the most delicate ways of using watercolour. It can be very sensitive and detailed. First, I did the drawing – as though it were to be a drawing in its own right. Naturally, the amount of detail you put in depends upon your drawing ability. All the shading was done with a pencil. Washes of colour were applied after the drawing was completed. Incidentally, this fixes the pencil and stops any smudging.

Pen and wash

A very popular technique, pen and wash is used at some time or another by many watercolour artists. The addition of the pen gives a sparkle to the painting. I painted the picture first, then added the pen work, but you can work the other way round – pen first – if you find it suits you better. Like body colour, the use of the pen is another method of saving a watercolour. Next time you want to put a bit more sparkle into a painting, try using a pen – you could transform a mediocre painting into a masterpiece.

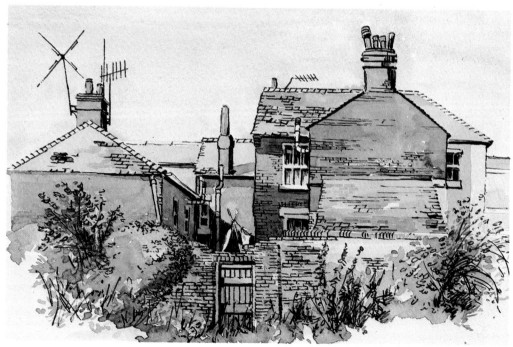

Pen and wash

Greens Pasteless Board 300lb HP

SIMPLE EXERCISES

No doubt you have had a few funny experiences with the paint. At times, you may have lost control or found that runs of paint have broken away from the main wash and run down the paper on to the table or the floor. However, you will have learned a lot and now, you can use this knowledge to do some real painting.

If you have been using cartridge paper or thin watercolour paper and have not yet tried stretching any paper, now is the time to do so. It makes an incredible difference, especially to cartridge paper. You will need to refer to the instructions on page 14.

Before you start a watercolour painting, you must always have *clean* water in your container. Remember, the paint stains the water to make the colour. If the water is dirty, obviously, you will not get a true, clear colour.

To avoid breaking my rhythm when I am painting in the studio, I sometimes speed up the drying time of a wash by using my wife's hair drier to blow dry my wash. If you do this, *don't hold the drier too close* – what you are trying to achieve is a *quicker*, *natural* way of drying your wash.

I have chosen a potato for the first exercise. The drawing is not too difficult and if you put a bump in the wrong place, it will not look wrong. Also, although the colour isn't bright or exciting, it can be easily matched. The colour of potatoes varies, so if you don't match it exactly, your painting will still look right. You may now have the impression that if an object isn't represented correctly, it doesn't matter. Of course, this is not true. What I am trying to do is to make sure that your first painting of an object looks correct to your family and friends so that you will receive their praise and congratulations. This will boost your confidence which, in turn, will improve your work. Now you can understand why I chose a potato for you – because it has no specific shape or colour.

First, draw the potato with your HB pencil. Using your large, round brush, paint the background as a wash. When this is dry, paint the potato and add more colour on the shadow side as you paint down. Before this paint is dry, use the same brush and darker colour to work the dark blemishes. Because the paint is still slightly wet, these marks will run a little and the edges will be soft. While the paint is still wet on the potato, dry out your brush and wipe out some highlights. These are only subtle effects but they help to give the object form. Finally, put in the shadow. Don't be fussy with the detail and, if it doesn't work out the first time, keep trying. When you can paint that potato, you will have come a long, long way. Try some more vegetables – you will find that you enjoy painting them.

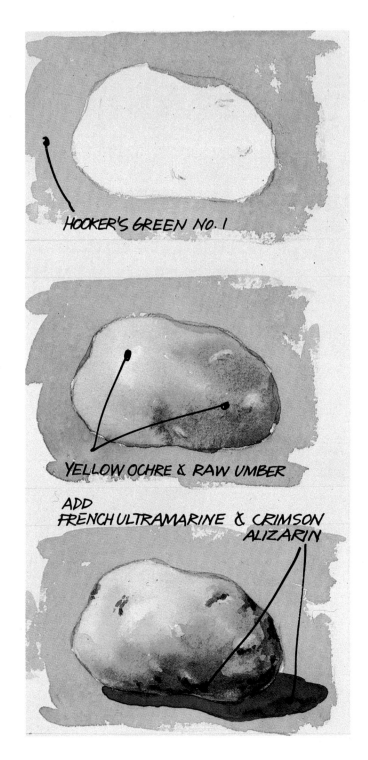

HOOKER'S GREEN NO. 1

YELLOW OCHRE & RAW UMBER

ADD FRENCH ULTRAMARINE & CRIMSON ALIZARIN

Complicated subject and simplified painting

Below is a complicated, pencil sketch I made of the River Hamble in Hampshire. I put quite a lot of drawing into this but, if you only wanted to paint it, you could manage by sketching only the key positions – the horizon, the wooden quay and a couple of the main boats – the brush could do the rest. I used a rough surface for this, a lot of dry brush, and I scratched out the light on the middle-distance water with a blade.

Complicated subject

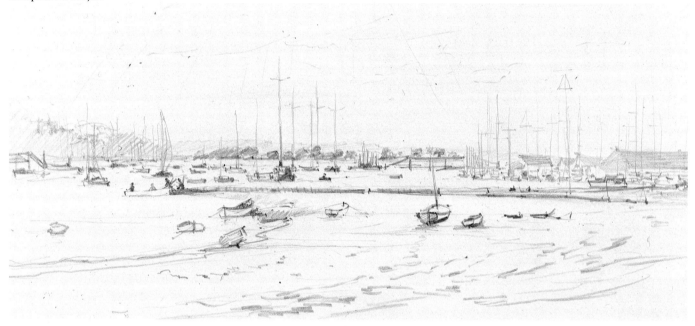

Simplified painting

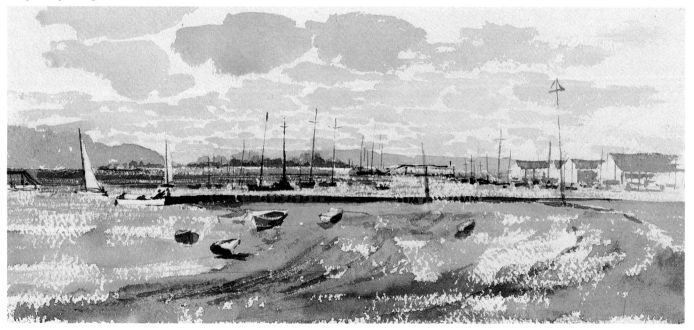

LET'S TRY A BANANA – USE THESE COLOURS   CADMIUM YELLOW PALE
BURNT UMBER
CRIMSON ALIZARIN
FRENCH ULTRAMARINE

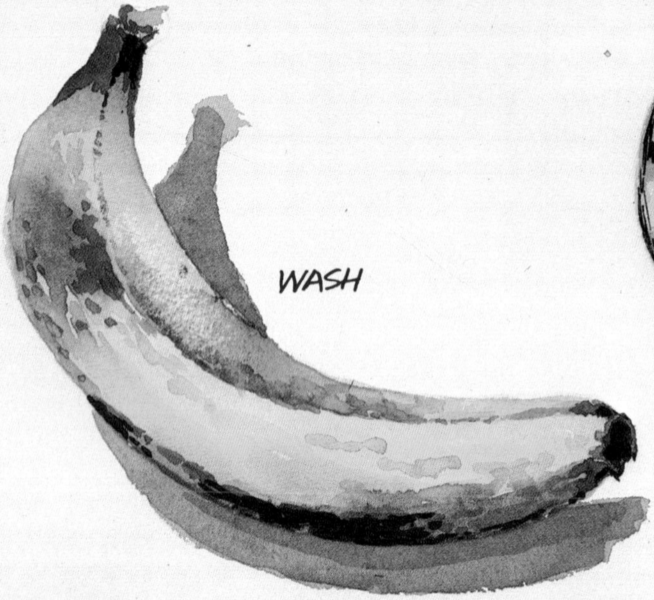

WASH

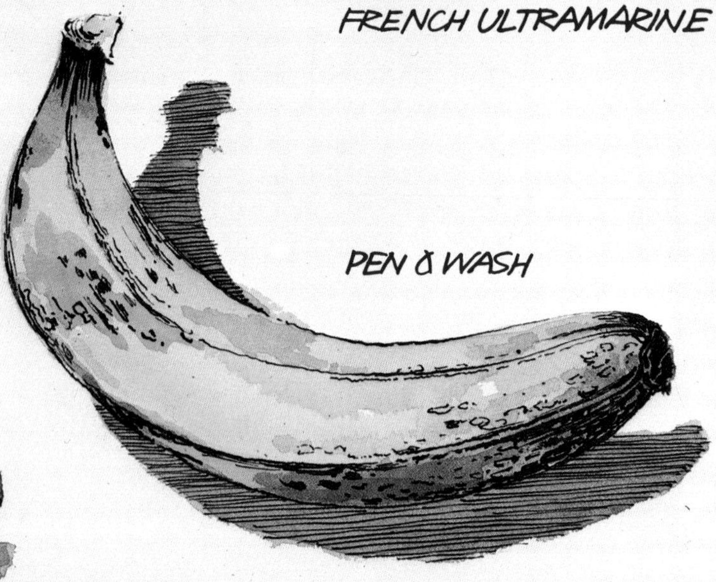

PEN & WASH

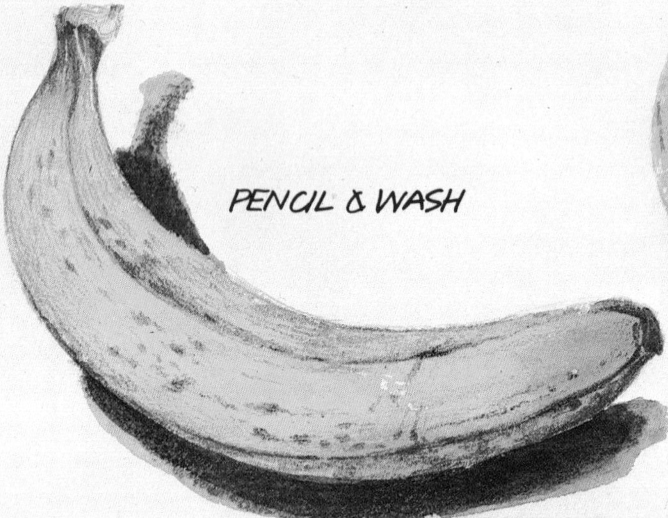

PENCIL & WASH

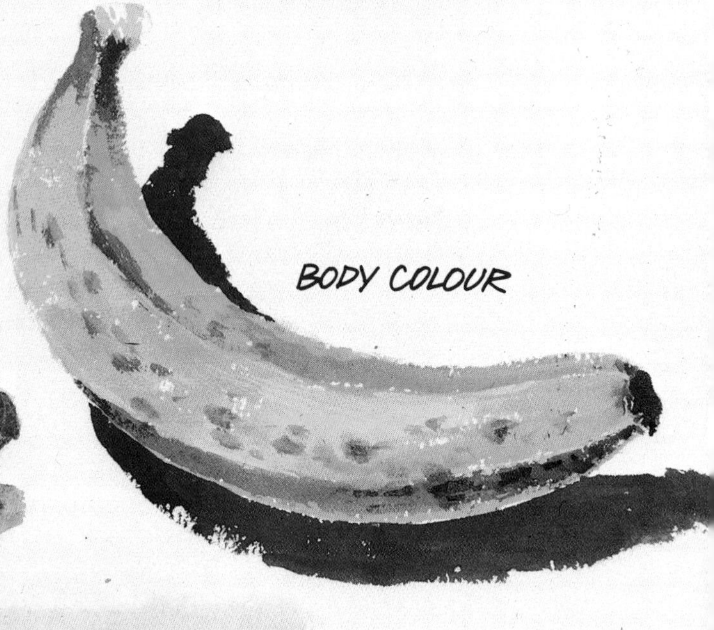

BODY COLOUR

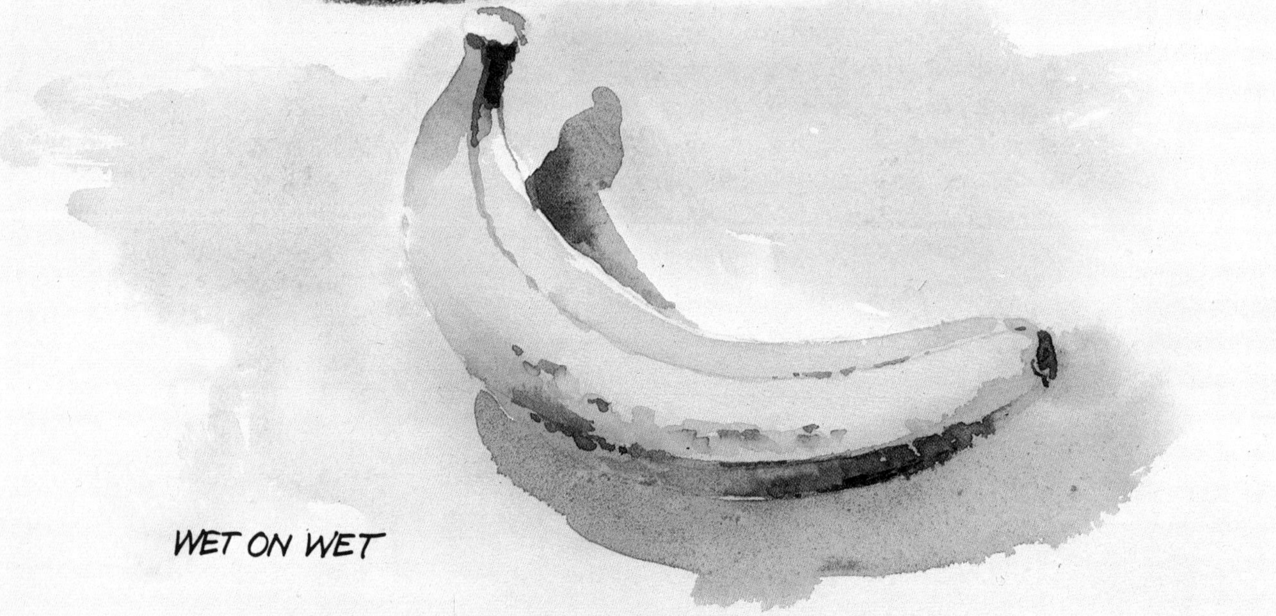

WET ON WET

Let's try a banana

This time, try a *very simple approach* to five of the techniques I described earlier. First, draw five bananas on the same sheet of paper with your HB pencil.

Now, paint the banana shapes, using the same colours for all five. Paint the first one, using your large, round brush and the colours shown. Let the brush strokes follow the shape of the banana. When the paint is almost dry, put on a darker wash and add some darker marks on top of this. Then, paint a dark shadow wash to show up the banana (light against dark). Put in a few dark accents with your small, size No. 6 brush to crispen it up.

Paint the pen and wash banana in the same way. When the wash is dry, use a mapping pen and black Indian ink to draw the banana. Experiment to find your natural style. You can try drawing the banana with pen and ink first before putting coloured washes over the top.

The next one is pencil and wash. Draw and shade the banana with your HB and 2B pencils as if you were doing a pencil drawing. Pencil leads are graded up to 6B (the softest, or blackest) so if you want darker shading on your drawing, use a softer pencil. Next, paint it in the same way as the first one but this time, over your pencil shading. Now, use the wet on wet technique. Use your sponge or large brush to wet the paper then, while it is still quite wet, paint the banana with the same brush. The colours will run over the edges of your pencil drawing. Then paint the darker side and add some dark blemishes. When this is nearly dry, use the same brush to paint your background. Start at the left, above the banana, follow its top shape in one brush stroke, then work underneath it.

Finally, we will use the body colour technique, i.e. we will use White to make the paint lighter and opaque. Usually, poster colour or tubes of gouache colour are used and you must *wash it off your palette* when you have finished with it. If white paint gets accidentally mixed with watercolour and applied to paper, and you *put a wash* over the top (or even a very watery brush), it will run and ruin your work. Now, paint your banana; using the same colours as before but adding White to them – don't use a lot of water. You will find that the paint does not flow so easily and you have to work it more than usual.

Now a rose

Use your size No. 6 brush to put a wash of Crimson Alizarin and Cadmium Red on the flower. While this is still wet, wipe out some of the paint for highlights with a damp brush. Paint the stem and leaves and, while the leaves are still wet, add some Cadmium Red with the point of the brush. Paint the petals with stronger colour and, when dry, scratch out some highlights. With the same brush, paint the background – very wet. Be definite when painting up to the leaves – let the brush stroke make the shape. Add some shadow on the stem and leaves under the flower.

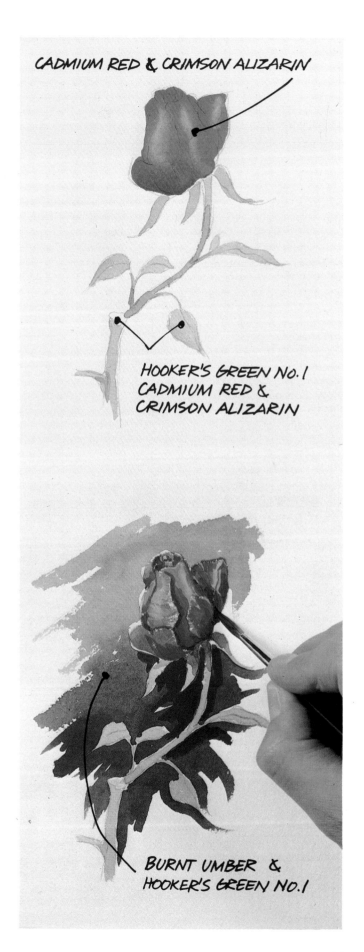

CADMIUM RED & CRIMSON ALIZARIN

HOOKER'S GREEN No. 1
CADMIUM RED &
CRIMSON ALIZARIN

BURNT UMBER &
HOOKER'S GREEN No. 1

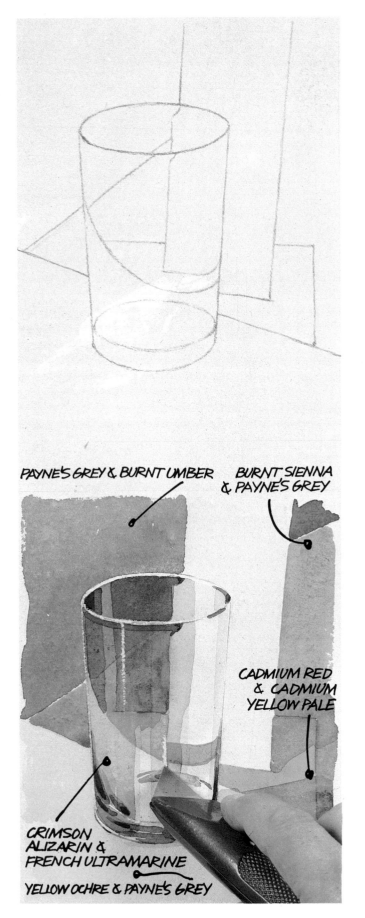

PAYNE'S GREY & BURNT UMBER

BURNT SIENNA & PAYNE'S GREY

CADMIUM RED & CADMIUM YELLOW PALE

CRIMSON ALIZARIN & FRENCH ULTRAMARINE

YELLOW OCHRE & PAYNE'S GREY

A drinking glass

I find that most students fight shy of painting glass and I am often asked how to make it look like *glass*. The answer, as always, is by *observation*. Look right through the glass and analyse the shapes behind it. Then, draw the glass and simplify these shapes. If you look at my drawing, you will see that definite shapes are formed *in* the glass. Use a large brush to paint the top-left, dark area first – leave the rim of the glass and paint into the glass. Then paint the orange areas. Next, use a very pale wash for the white areas, leaving some unpainted white paper in the glass. Now, using downward strokes, put a dark wash down the left-hand side of the glass, leaving some areas untouched. When this is dry, go over the area again with even darker colour and add a few dark accents with your small sable brush. Use a sharp blade to scratch out some highlights on the glass.

Set up your own glass and study the background shapes – I am sure you will soon learn the secret of painting a glass.

Now some skies

I have already said that the wash is the basis of all water-colour painting and if you have been practising your basic techniques, you should now be able to handle a wash quite confidently. The last two exercises – a rose and a glass – needed a lot of hard thinking and careful brush work but you can be a little more relaxed when painting skies. After all, if you get the overall shape of a cloud correct, it doesn't matter if you have an extra bump here and there. Skies are one of the best subjects on which to practise washes and large brush work, and although it is an exercise, you can produce a very rewarding painting.

Tackle this exercise for the sheer joy of painting and enjoy the freedom that the paint and the subject matter allow. My six paintings were all done on Greens Pasteless Board 300lb Not but you can try all kinds of paper, surfaces, weights, colours, and so on. I worked them exactly twice the size they are reproduced here, i.e. 18cm (7in) wide – a handy size on which to practise this exercise because you have more control over the paint on a small area.

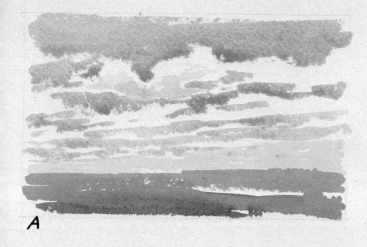

A

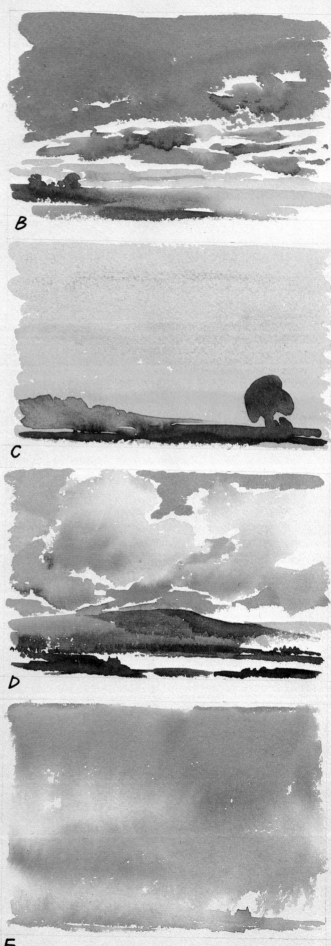

B

C

D

E

A This was a clear, windy day and the clouds were moving across the sky quite fast. I used dry paper and a size No. 10 brush. First, I painted a wash of Coeruleum Blue and a little Crimson Alizarin for the blue sky then, while it was wet, I added Yellow Ochre to the mix and used it for the shadow of the clouds

B Here, I applied a wash of Payne's Grey, French Ultramarine and Crimson Alizarin to dry paper with a size No. 10 brush, leaving white areas for clouds. While this was wet, I painted the darker sides of the clouds. Then, I added a touch of Yellow Ochre to the dark shadows

C This evening sky has a normal graded wash worked from the top to the horizon, and below the land. The paper was dry and I used Coeruleum Blue, Crimson Alizarin and Cadmium Yellow Pale for the wash, worked with a size No. 10 brush

D These big, full clouds were painted first with a mixture of Yellow Ochre, Crimson Alizarin and French Ultramarine. Before they dried, French Ultramarine mixed with Crimson Alizarin (blue sky) was painted between them, leaving white edges – a silver lining to help merge the clouds. Notice the little silhouette of a cottage at the bottom left and the white lake at the foot of the hills – this gives dimension to the clouds

E A very wet, drizzly day, The paper was soaked with a sponge except at the bottom, right-hand corner. A mix of French Ultramarine, Crimson Alizarin, Payne's Grey and Yellow Ochre was worked on to the wet paper and you can see the result. Where the paper was dry at the bottom right, I let the brush form the cottage – again, to give atmosphere and dimension

F For this evening sky I applied a normal wash of Crimson Alizarin and Cadmium Yellow Pale over the paper. When the wash was dry I painted the clouds, using a size No. 6 brush and with French Ultramarine added to the colour. Before these clouds were dry, I worked a darker wash over them to form the dark clouds just above the horizon

F

EXERCISE ONE
STILL LIFE

On the following pages I have taken nine subjects and worked them in stages for you to follow, and copy if you wish. I have explained how to do the work and, most important, I have shown the same painting from the first stage to the last (the finished stage). This is important because you see the *same painting* through its stages and you can look back to see what was done earlier. It is also important for you to know the size of the finished painting (not the reproduction) because this gives you a relative scale to adjust to. The actual size is indicated under the finished stage.

The close-up illustrations for each exercise are reproduced the same size as I painted them so that you can see the actual brush strokes and details. Finally, I have used insets to illustrate the method of painting passages that I think you need to see more closely.

For your first exercise I have purposely chosen a still life subject because the objects are easy to find but, above all, they can be painted under your own conditions. This is the beauty of still life: you can control the lighting, size, shape and colour of your subject. If you use inorganic objects, you can paint the same ones for years. To avoid your spending that long on your still life, I have added some fruit.

Before we start, here are one or two important notes on still-life painting. Don't be too ambitious to start with. Set up just a few objects that have simple shapes and colours, and put them on a contrasting background. The best light source is an adjustable desk lamp which can be directed on to your subject to give maximum light and shade (light against dark). Before you set up a still life subject, make sure that none of the objects you use will be needed by you or your family in the near future.

First stage Draw the picture with an HB pencil. Using your large brush, mix Hooker's Green No. 1, Crimson Alizarin and French Ultramarine, and paint a wash down the paper, working around the fruit but painting over the left-hand side of the glass jar. Now, work a wash down the right-hand side of the picture, using French Ultramarine, Crimson Alizarin and Yellow Ochre – again, paint over the jar but leave some white paper for highlights. Paint the table top with the same colour.

Second stage Paint the sultanas in the jar, using Crimson Alizarin, French Ultramarine and Cadmium Yellow Pale. While the paint is still wet, dry your brush and wipe out the two highlights on the jar. Then start putting in the fruit. Load your brush with watery paint and start with the orange – use Cadmium Yellow Pale, Cadmium Red and a touch of French Ultramarine in the shadow area. Next, paint the apple with Hooker's Green No. 1 and Cadmium Yellow Pale. Add the red lines of the apples while the paint is still wet so that they will merge and look softer. Paint the two pears with a wash of Cadmium Yellow Pale and Hooker's Green No. 1. When they are nearly dry, paint the darker, browny-green areas with Hooker's Green No. 1, Crimson Alizarin and Yellow Ochre. The onion is next: use Cadmium Yellow Pale and Crimson Alizarin. With a wash of Yellow Ochre and Burnt Umber, paint all the nuts inside and outside the bowl, except the kernel inside the broken walnut. When these are dry, add Crimson Alizarin to your wash to give more tone to the chestnuts. Dry out the highlights with your brush. Paint the blue dish, using French Ultramarine and a little Hooker's Green No. 1; add more pigment to the wash so that it gets darker to the right of the bowl – make sure you leave a white rim to the bowl.

Third stage By now, all the areas have a wash over them but no detail or depth is apparent. At this stage, darker washes are applied to the painting. Start with the green background, using the same colours but adding more pigment. Paint over the jar again but *do leave some areas of the original wash* showing. As you work on the fruit, use a little more brush work to achieve moulding and shape.

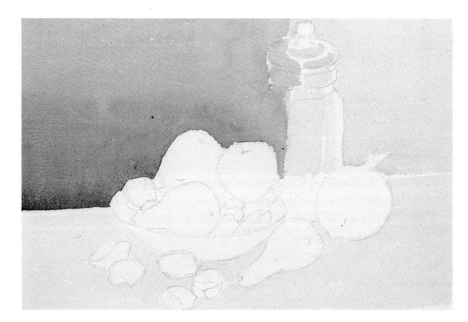

First stage

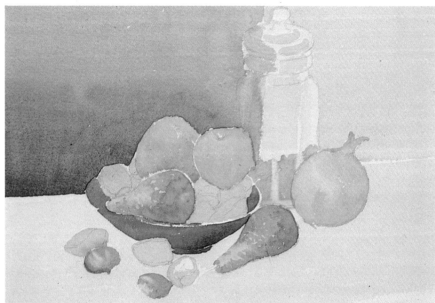

Second stage

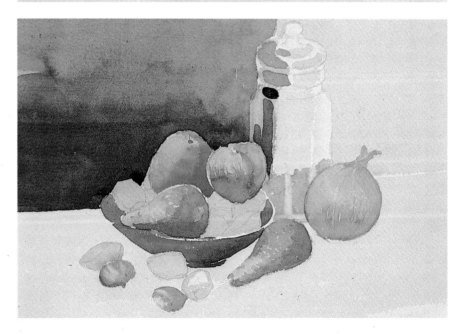

Third stage

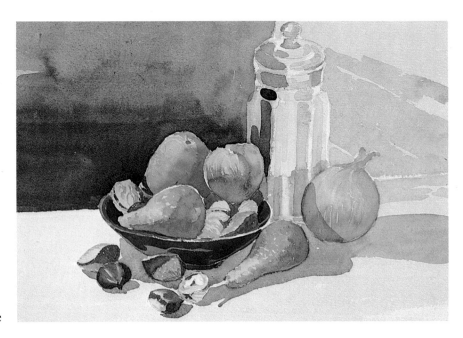

Fourth stage

Fourth stage Now your work on the nuts begins in earnest. Use your size No. 6 brush and start with the walnuts. Let the brush do the drawing of the gnarled shells, as if it were a pencil. If you find the line too harsh or too strong, dry your brush and soften the line with it. Work the brazil nuts and the chestnuts in the same way. Whatever you do, keep the highlights on the chestnuts – they are an essential feature of these particular nuts. Now paint the shadows with a wash of Crimson Alizarin, French Ultramarine and Yellow Ochre; when these are dry, add another wash to the bowl. Finally, use one stroke to put a wash down the right-hand side of the jar and over the sultanas.

Finished stage The picture is almost finished at this stage but it lacks that final crispness and a little detail. This work is done with a size No. 6 brush. Start with the jar, adding dark line-work to give it better definition. Wipe some colour off the left-hand side of the apple to accentuate its shape and to separate it from the orange. Then, add the stalk. Paint some thin lines on the onion and work the sultanas in the jar in more detail. Give all the nuts stronger treatment and paint the shadows cast from the apple and pear on the nuts in the bowl. Put some stippling on the orange with your size No. 6 brush for an orange-skin look – use darker paint and work from the dark area into the light, leaving light areas showing through (see below). Finally, paint all the shadows again with a stronger wash.

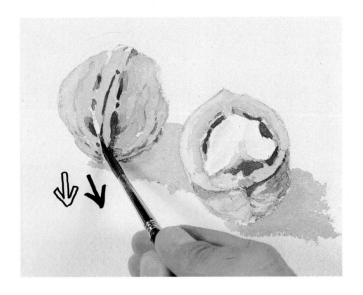

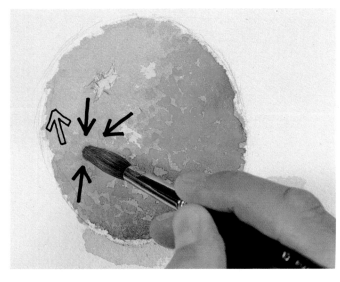

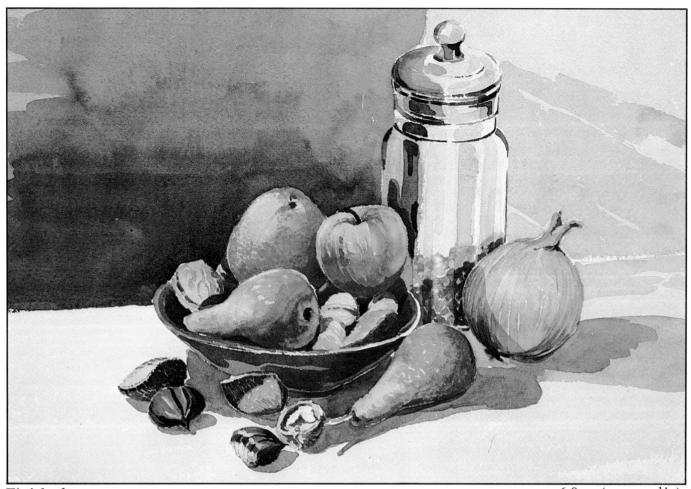

Finished stage
$25.3 \times 36.8\text{cm} \ (10 \times 14\frac{1}{2}\text{in})$

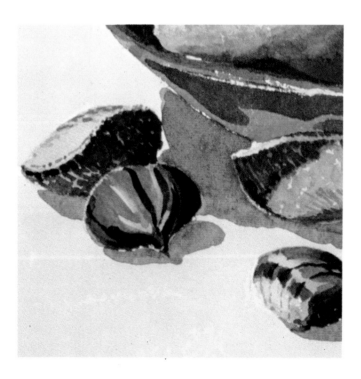

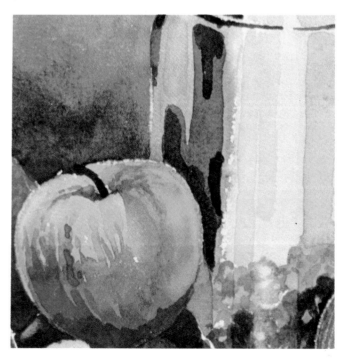

EXERCISE TWO
FLOWERS

This exercise, also, is one that can be controlled to a large degree by the artist. The main point to remember is that flowers change over a short period and eventually die. Therefore, any flowers that you use as a subject must be capable of outstaying your painting time. If you don't manage to finish in time, change the flowers for fresh ones; your painting should have progressed far enough for you to improvise. Remember, you are expressing an impression of a flower, not a *specific* one. A vase of different blooms with exciting shapes and colours can be a tremendous inspiration and make a fine painting. It can also be a daunting prospect for the beginner and if attempted at an early stage, can lead to disaster and disappointment. Remember: walk before you can run.

At first, study one species and only one bloom at a time. Put one flower against a plain, contrasting background so that you can see it clearly. Observe its characteristics: study how the petals are formed, their shape, how it grows from the stem and, just as important, study the leaves. When you have mastered a certain flower, put some in a vase and paint away. You will find it helpful, at times, to use other colours in addition to those in your watercolour box because the colours of flowers are infinite. For this exercise I have chosen flowers that can be painted with the colours I normally use and which have been used throughout this book.

First stage I have painted these flowers in a much looser style than the still life. I have used a much broader treatment and have not worried as much about detail. The vase, in particular, I worked with deliberate brush strokes, allowing the brush to do the drawing and shadowing at the same time (see below). You must get yourself into the right frame of mind to start this painting. It is not one to be worked on for days; it should be very direct and unlaboured. The same colours are used for the flowers throughout the five stages. They are: for the yellow chrysanthemum, Cadmium Yellow Pale, not quite pure – add just a touch of Crimson Alizarin; for the red and orange flowers, Crimson Alizarin and a touch of Cadmium Yellow Pale; for the shadow of the white flowers, Coeruleum Blue and Crimson Alizarin. Draw the flowers and the vase with an HB pencil. Next, soak the paper with your sponge and prepare plenty of watery paint in your palette. First, use your large, round brush to paint the yellow flower in the centre, then the top yellow flower, the two left-hand ones, the shadow areas of the white flowers and, finally, the orange and red ones. You will find that the colours run and merge; this is intentional – we are really starting with a wet on wet technique.

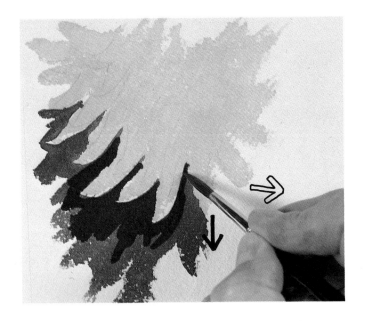

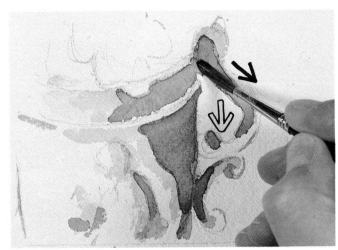

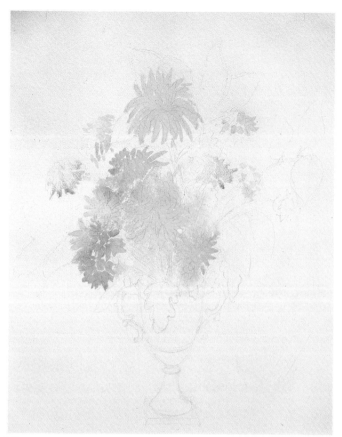

First stage

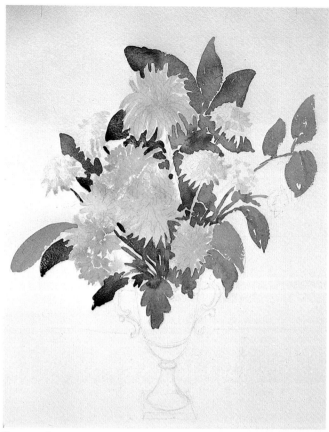

Second stage

Second stage Mix plenty of watery paint in your palette, using Hooker's Green No. 1, Payne's Grey and Crimson Alizarin. Still using your large brush, paint the leaves and stems. As you draw the leaves with your brush you will find that some of them run into each other – again, this is correct. Vary the density and colour of the leaves as you work; this helps to give light and shade to these dark areas. Work freely into the petals of the flowers but make sure that the petals are formed in the right direction.

Third stage Work the vase next, using a very wet, loaded brush. Paint the handles and moulding, using French Ultramarine, Crimson Alizarin and Yellow Ochre. If you look at the third stage illustration, you will see how the wet paint formed a natural, long blob at the bottom of the right-hand handle's curve. Now, add more Yellow Ochre to your mix and paint the background, still using your large brush and working very wet from the top downwards. Go over some of the leaves – this will help to give them a little more depth and variation. You can now see the shapes of the white flowers on the right. Put in the shadows cast by the vase on the base, using the same colours that you used for the background.

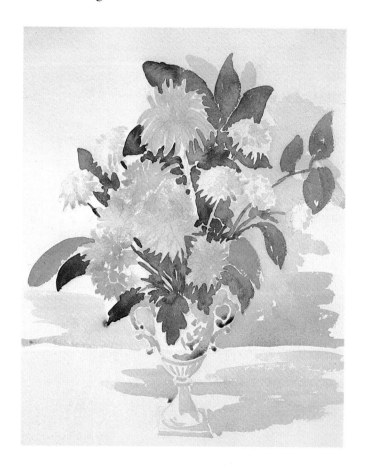

Third stage

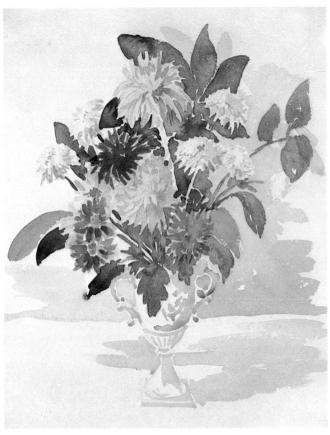

Fourth stage

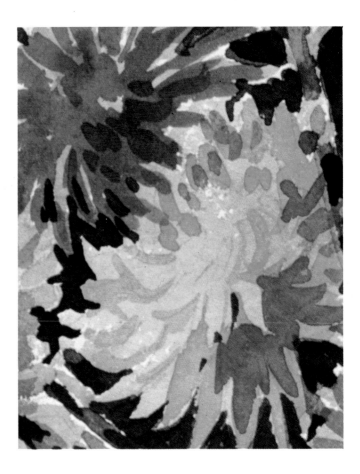

Fourth stage You now need to work over the flowers to add more colour and form. Use the same flower colours that you started with but use more pigment (keep the colour watery but *very* much stronger). Use your size No. 6 brush to draw the petals on the flowers, letting the brush strokes form the petals. Keep the colour of the paint strong, your brush wet, and your brush strokes free – don't get involved with detail. Where you want a little more dark on the red flower, add a little French Ultramarine.

Finished stage When using this watercolour technique, if you go too far or put in too much detail at this stage, your picture will lose its charm and freshness. Still using your size No. 6 brush, very wet, paint over the inner leaves and main stem, working the dark colour between the petal shapes again to give the final accent (light against dark). You will notice that the two white blooms, top right, appear to be much whiter. This is a typical example of the light against dark principle. Also, the leaf overhanging the vase is much more pronounced, now that it has been painted again. Add some more dark washes to the vase, to give it more definition and to help pull it off the background.

You will find that certain watercolour techniques can only be executed well when the artist is in key with that particular technique. For instance, if you are feeling on top of the world and uninhibited, then this flower exercise or the landscape (a later exercise) are the very paintings to work on. On the other hand, if you are feeling cosy, secure and mellow, then you will execute the detailed work in, say, the still life or the pencil and wash drawing very much better at that particular time. Remember, the painting comes from your mind, through your arm and hand, into your brush. If you choose the right technique at the right time, you will get the best out of yourself.

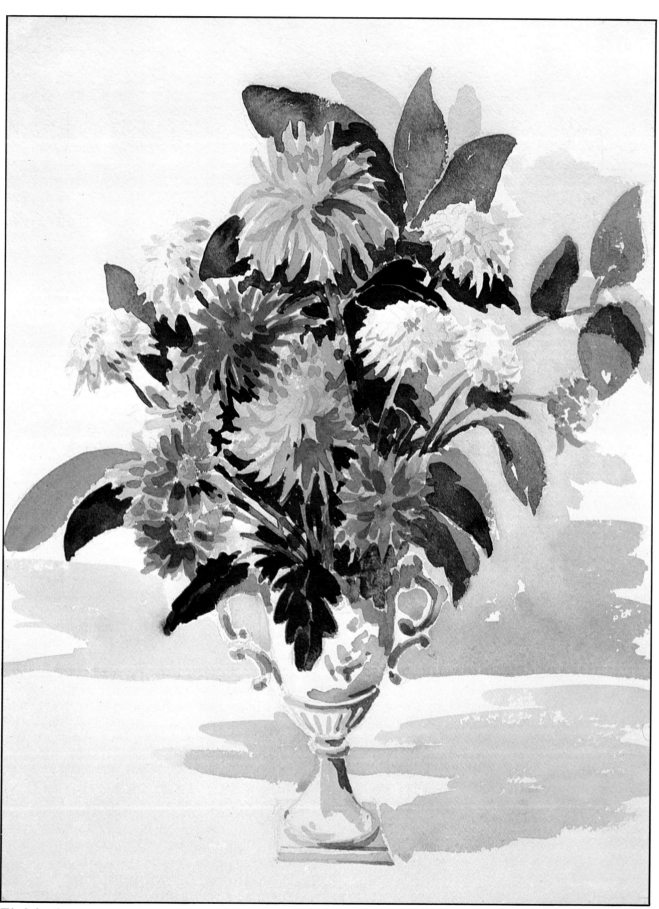

Finished stage

44.4 × 33cm (17½ × 13in)

EXERCISE THREE
PORTRAIT

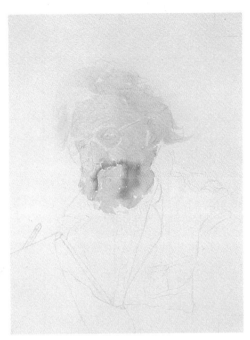

First stage

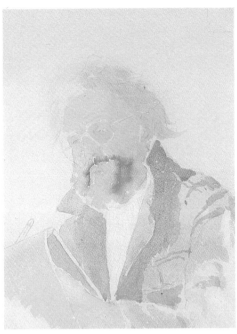

Second stage

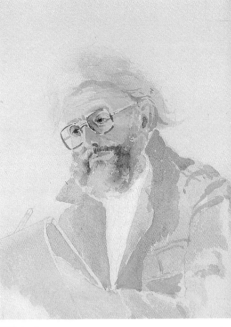

Third stage

For the student, portrait painting has many advantages in common with still life and flower painting. You can dictate the lighting, colour scheme and mood. The painting of a portrait does not depend on the weather but only on your model's availability. But, remember, you always have one model with you – yourself; all you need is a mirror.

Watercolour is not the easiest of mediums to use for portraits but it does have some natural advantages. With watercolour, you can create an impression of the subject that has a very fresh and unlaboured appearance. Also, washes can be used in some very delicate work to give depth to the skin tones. If you find that you start to lose it while working on a portrait, carry on with body colour, or even pen work, and you may find that you have succeeded in painting a good portrait. The likeness can come through as an impression – a feeling. If you want detail, eventually, then you can gradually build up to it through practice and careful observation.

First stage Draw the portait with an HB pencil. Wet the paper with a sponge and wait until it is nearly dry (when the shine has gone). Then, using your large brush, mix Coeruleum Blue and Crimson Alizarin, and paint the hair, leaving an area unpainted above the forehead. While this is still wet, use Cadmium Red and Yellow Ochre to paint the first wash of the flesh tones, letting this colour mix with the hair. Use a stronger wash (add Crimson Alizarin and a touch of French Ultramarine to your first wash) to paint the shadow side of the face. This will mix with the wash underneath and keep the edges soft. While it is still wet, paint the beard, using Payne's Grey and Crimson Alizarin.

Second stage Now, paint the jacket with a mix of Coeruleum Blue and Crimson Alizarin. While it is still damp add Payne's Grey to your wash and put in the shadows. Paint the wrist and the shadow of the sketching pad.

Third stage More detail is to be added to the face in this stage. Use your size No. 6 brush and the same colours as in the first two stages but mix them stronger. If you get a hard line you can soften it by stroking it with a damp brush. If it is difficult to move, wet the area with your brush and blot up the surface water with blotting paper. (Always keep

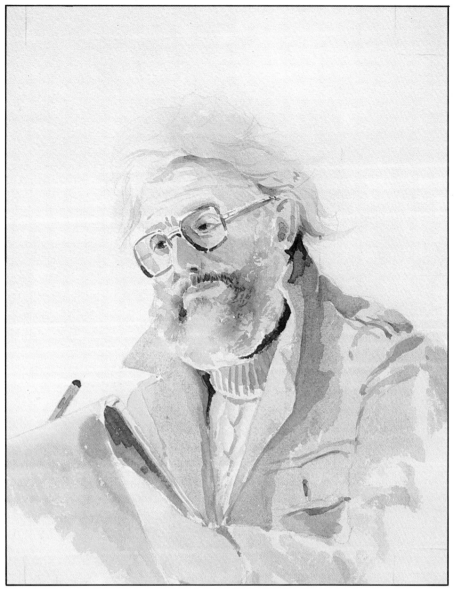

Finished stage   32.3 × 24.7cm (12¾ × 9¾in)

blotting paper at your side – it is invaluable for getting you out of trouble.) When the face is really dry, use French Ultramarine and Crimson Alizarin to paint the glasses, leaving some areas unpainted for highlights.

Finished stage The last stage involves crispening up your painting and adding the jumper. Draw this with a brush, using French Ultramarine, Crimson Alizarin and Yellow Ochre. Now, use your size No. 6 brush and a mix of French Ultramarine, Crimson Alizarin and Yellow Ochre: put the dark accents under the right side of the beard, to the left of the jumper, at the back of the jacket collar, under the jacket lapel; draw some detail around the jacket pocket and put the shadow on the pad. Finally, put a small accent under the hair and paint the pencil.

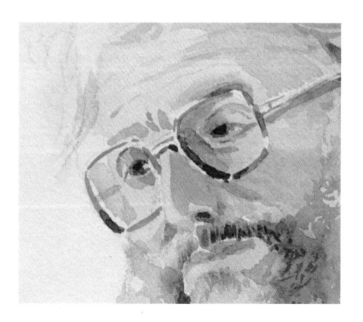

EXERCISE FOUR
LANDSCAPE

Landscape painting holds the romantic promise of a day spent in the countryside painting away, enjoying ourselves to the full. This applies to many artists but not to all: some people worry about painting while strangers look on, others can't get out into the countryside as often as they would like to. If you lack confidence, the best way to start is to tuck yourself away behind a tree, make a quick drawing in your sketch book of a scene you would like to paint and mark the main colours in pencil, then paint it at home. As your confidence grows, take your watercolour box outside with you. Remember that nine out of ten people who take the trouble to come to see you will be full of admiration for you and your work.

Sketching in pencil also applies to the person who can't often get outside. Rather than always *painting* just one scene when you *do* go out, instead make a few different pencil sketches. Six of them could be completed in a day. Take your watercolour box and some water with you, and make some colour notes on these sketches. Then, when it's stay-at-home day, you can use this information to produce six different paintings.

A landscape can be painted from a window, if necessary, but you must sketch and paint outside as much as possible. Always carry a sketch book with you; even if you only have ten minutes to sketch a scene and draw only ten lines, you will have had to observe it. The important factor is *observation*. The knowledge it provides will be committed to your memory and you will find that, in time, you will be capable of painting from memory indoors. Those memory banks must be kept in good condition – take every opportunity to observe and sketch out-of-doors.

I have chosen this landscape for working the wet on wet technique; this gives the real, wet, watercolour look. Remember to thoroughly soak your paper. Incidentally, I should warn you that once you start a painting like this you are committed to continue to the end while it is still wet or damp.

First stage I get a great deal of pleasure from using this watercolour technique, especially when worked to the extreme as it is in this exercise. It has an element of risk – where is the paint going? – and one of great excitement. Although you have planned in your mind what you want to do and you can control it to a great extent, there is the *certainty* of many a happy accident, and even pure surprise, when using this technique. For you to copy this picture, or even for me to copy it, and achieve the same result would be an impossibility. What you have to do is work towards the same composition and if a happy accident occurs, then use it. I will explain what to do, as I have in the other exercises, but remember, your painting will have its own little gems created purely by this wet on wet technique. Draw the picture with your HB pencil, using a minimum of drawing. Soak the paper thoroughly with water. Use your large brush and put on your palette French Ultramarine, Crimson Alizarin, Payne's Grey and Yellow Ochre – *don't* mix these colours all together in the palette; apply them to the wet paper and they will mix on the surface, creating some beautiful effects. Run the sky into the land and notice the unpainted area I left for the puddle.

Second stage Using a wash of Payne's Grey, Crimson Alizarin and Yellow Ochre, paint the middle-distance trees with your large brush. These will run into the sky and lose a bit of shape but don't worry, the impression you are creating is that of a landscape in an early-morning mist. While these trees are wet, paint the main trees into them. Then, using your size No. 6 brush, add some smaller branches. Next, take your large brush on to the now damp

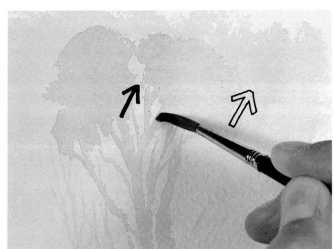

First stage

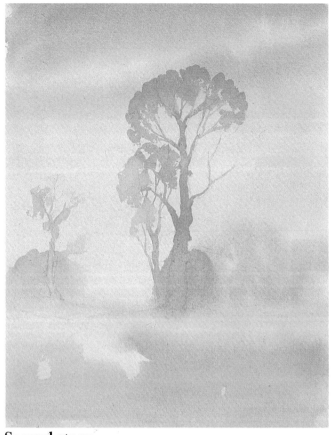

Second stage

sky and drag the brush down into the wet, small branches (so it all runs together) to form the top of the trees. If at any stage your work dries out too quickly for you, wet the paper again; it may move some of the pigment but if you do it gently, you will get away with it.

Third stage With your large brush and plenty of watery paint – Payne's Grey, Burnt Umber, Hooker's Green No. 1 and Crimson Alizarin – paint the foreground. You will notice that the puddle is more obvious, now that a darker tone has been added.

Third stage

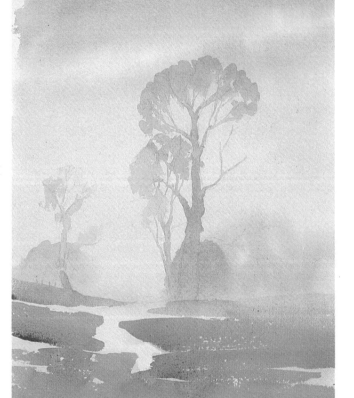

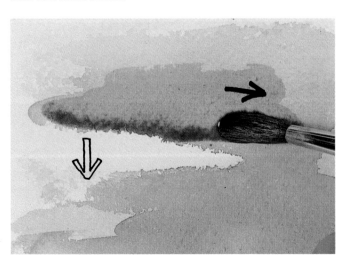

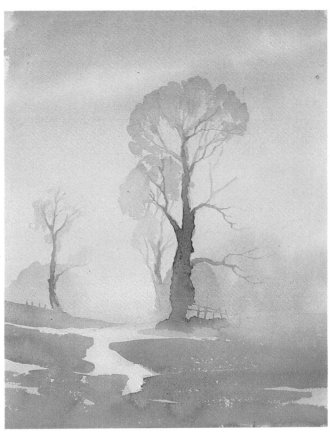

Fourth stage

Fourth stage Work over the main tree again while it is still damp. Use your size No. 6 brush to put in some more branches but keep them light in tone at the top. Also, paint the tree in the left-middle distance. Add the little bit of fence to the right of the main tree.

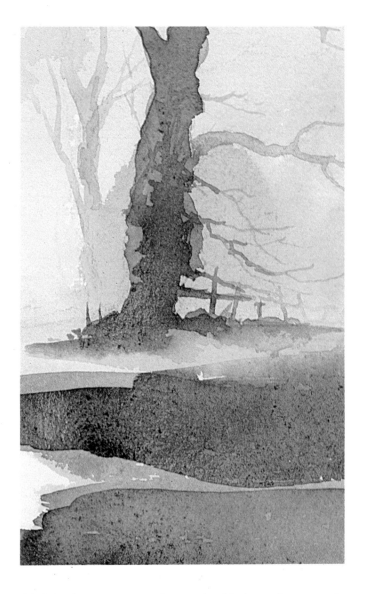

Finished stage Put another wash of darker colour over the foreground and add any darker accents you feel necessary for your picture. *Don't overdo the detail* when using this technique. I will give you some idea of timing on this type of picture: I took about 45 minutes to complete it. This effect cannot be achieved if you work slowly, the very essence of the technique is speed. Some artists use this technique to start a painting and then, when it has reached this stage (finished stage), they spend a lot of time working it up into a highly detailed watercolour – you could try that, next time.

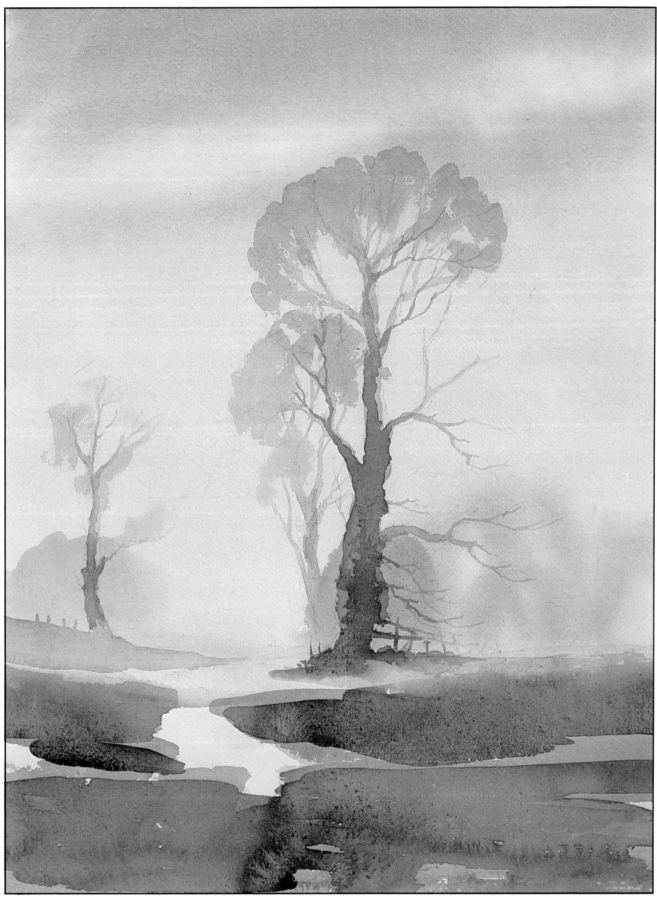

Finished stage

36.8 × 28cm (14½ × 11in)

EXERCISE FIVE
BUILDINGS

Buildings can be a tremendous source of pleasure to the artist. You may be inspired by the size and splendour of a building or by the quaint, old-world charm of a village street. Watercolour is a good medium to use for buildings, and buildings are a good subject for the student of watercolour. When you look at buildings with a painting in mind, you will see that the colour areas are broken up into quite definite shapes. In an earlier exercise, you looked through the drinking glass to find the shapes and colours; buildings have already done this for you. The shapes of roofs and walls, windows and doors, are quite definite and these shapes give you the areas on which to work your washes. But these are disciplined washes and different to those you used for the sky exercises.

A great deal of my watercolour training was done outside, sitting on the pavement, just off the main flow of people, painting buildings. If you are worried about sitting at the top of your local high street to paint, you can usually find some little corner where you can tuck yourself away, unnoticed. One of the great advantages of using watercolour to paint buildings is that you need only a small amount of equipment: stool, sketch block or some paper on a drawing board, paint box, brushes, water container, pencil and eraser. In fact, you don't always need a stool: sometimes, you can get a very good view of buildings from your car, in a car park. I have an estate car and I have often worked from that.

The subject of this exercise, I believe, is not too advanced and I have made it a pencil and wash drawing for those who can draw. If you feel you would rather stick to painting as a technique, you can do so. After drawing the main building areas simply work with your washes as you did in the still life exercise. Use the colours I suggest but mix them much stronger (I want the pencil to show through the wash).

First stage Draw the main area of the composition with an HB pencil, then draw the areas that you want to show through the washes. This means all-detail-work areas of tone and shadow. When shading, it is usually best to start at the top of the drawing to avoid working over finished, lower areas and smudging them. Start with the chimney and draw the stones, shading a few of them because some are darker than others. Work down on to the tiled roof, then the the lower part of the main building, drawing the stones again as you did on the chimney.

Second stage Continue drawing with your HB pencil, working next the houses at the end of the street – note that no stonework is drawn on these because this would make them appear nearer. Then, put in the house on the right, working plenty of shading on it because it is in shadow. Put plenty of pencil work on the lean-to against the main building, being very careful with the tiles and windows, and the railings in front of it. Draw the three figures and the shadow cast by the man in broad pencil shading. Add some dark accents with your 2B or 3B pencil. Now, you should have a drawing capable of standing in its own right as a pencil drawing.

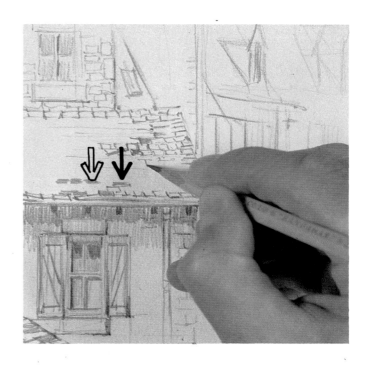

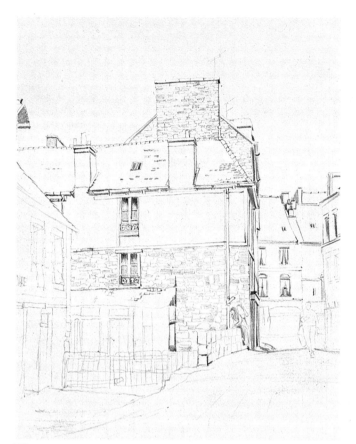

First stage

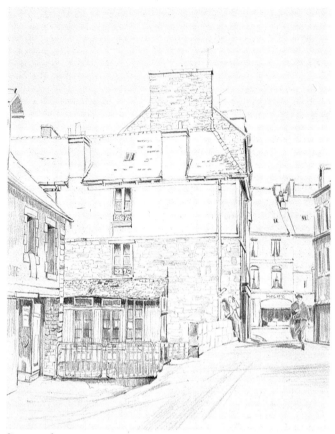

Second stage

Third stage For this exercise I used Greens Camber Sand 72lb Not paper. It was not stretched, only pinned to a drawing board. Incidentally, I used a piece of cartridge paper as a backing sheet in order to get a better line with the pencil; if you do not do this, the grain of the drawing board can be felt through the paper and will hinder the pencil lines. Because the paper is not very heavy, don't use very wet washes. Using your large brush, paint the sky with Coeruleum Blue and Crimson Alizarin. Be sure to keep all your washes well diluted so that they do not cover your pencil work. Your pencil must show through in order to achieve the full beauty of this effect. Next, paint the stonework, using Raw Umber, French Ultramarine and Crimson Alizarin.

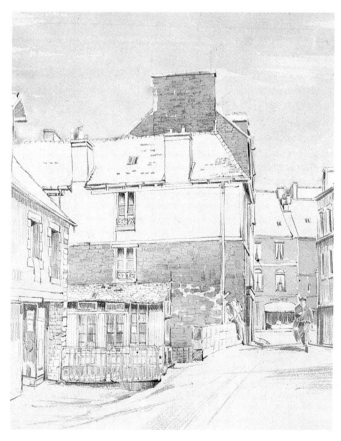

Third stage

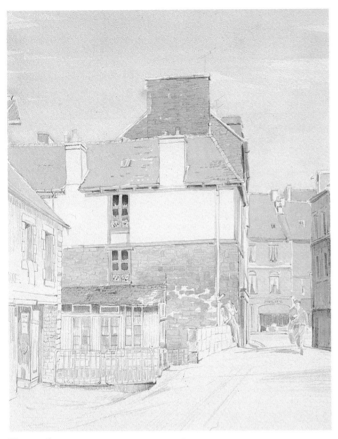

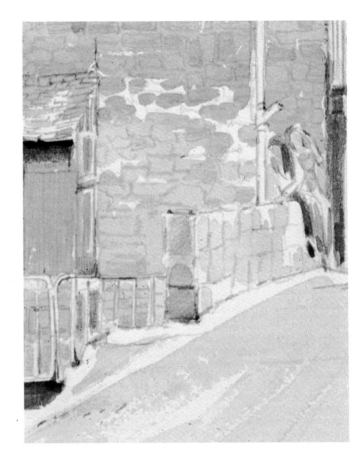

Fourth stage

Fourth stage Use a mixture of French Ultramarine, Crimson Alizarin and Raw Umber on the roofs. Paint the red tiles on top of the roofs with Cadmium Red and Cadmium Yellow Pale. Darken the mixture you used on the roofs and use this to work a wash on the windows. Put in the orange-painted, wooden beams on the main house and use the same colour for the window frames; put a dark stonework-coloured wash over the buildings on the right and, finally, paint the red canopy at the end of the street with a weak wash of Cadmium Red.

Finished stage Paint a wash of Burnt Sienna and Crimson Alizarin over the lean-to extension, then use French Ultramarine and Crimson Alizarin to paint over the windows and the dark wall under the railings. Put a wash on the windows of the left-hand house and add a tone of Yellow Ochre, Crimson Alizarin and French Ultramarine over the front of the house. Put a dark tone on the figure and a broad, dark accent down the right of the two figures against the main house. Apply a wash of French Ultramarine, Crimson Alizarin and Yellow Ochre to the road with your size No. 6 brush, using broad strokes. With the same brush, add any dark accents you feel necessary.

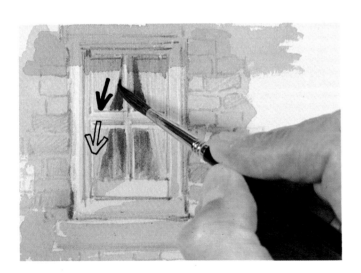

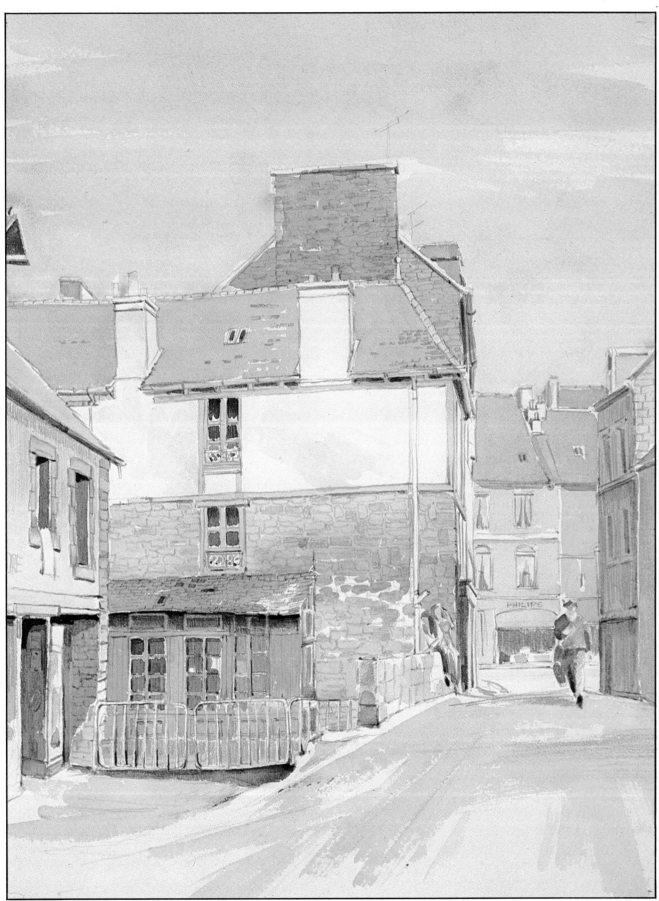

Finished stage

$36.8 \times 28\text{cm} \left(14\frac{1}{2} \times 11\text{in}\right)$

EXERCISE SIX
WATER

First stage

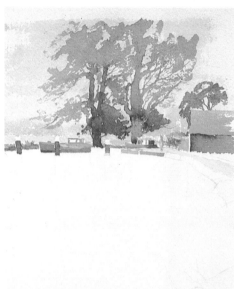

Second stage

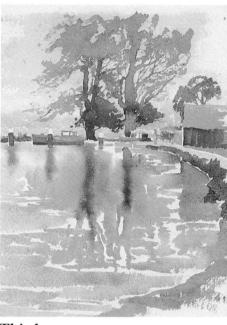

Third stage

A lake or pond (unless discoloured by mud) reflects its immediate surroundings and the sky. In very clear, still water the reflection of a building can be mirror-like; therefore, the water is painted as a building, upside-down. This is important: the reflection goes *down* vertically into the water, not across the surface. It is only the movement of the water that shows as horizontal lines and, remember, any movement breaks up the reflected images. Light on moving water is also seen horizontally. The first, golden rule for painting water is to make sure that all movement lines or shapes are *perfectly horizontal*. If they are not, you will have painted a sloping river or lake.

The illusion of water can be created quite simply with watercolour. Even leaving white paper to suggest water can be very effective (remember example D on page 33 when you were practising skies – the lake with the silhouette of the cottage at the side is white paper). Painting reflections can be approached in the same way as painting the glass. Observe your subject carefully and decide what the main shapes and colours are. Then go ahead.

A very wet on wet technique is usually very descriptive of water. Learn to observe the different moods of water and remember that a reflection immediately creates the illusion of water.

First stage Before you paint water, the surroundings must be painted first because these determine the colour and the shapes on the water. Draw the picture with you HB pencil but don't draw on the water area, these shapes will be created with your brush. Wet the paper with a sponge, then paint a wash of Coeruleum Blue and Crimson Alizarin. Just before it is dry, put in the middle-distance trees with French Ultramarine, Crimson Alizarin and Hooker's Green No. 1. Paint the field underneath, using Cadmium Yellow Pale and a little Crimson Alizarin. Next, paint the roof of the boat-house with Cadmium Red, Cadmium Yellow Pale and Hooker's Green No. 1.

Second stage Paint the mooring posts and side of the boat-house, using Payne's Grey and Hooker's Green No. 1. Then paint the tree trunks, working upwards with your large brush and using Payne's Grey, Hooker's Green No. 1 and Burnt Umber. While the trunks are still wet, paint into these with Cadmium Yellow Pale, Hooker's Green No. 1 and Crimson Alizarin to form the leaves. Do this with your size No. 6 brush, making diagonal strokes from right to left at a flattish angle to the paper. You will get a broad, hit-and-miss stroke which will give the impression of leaves. Paint the boats and bank of the river.

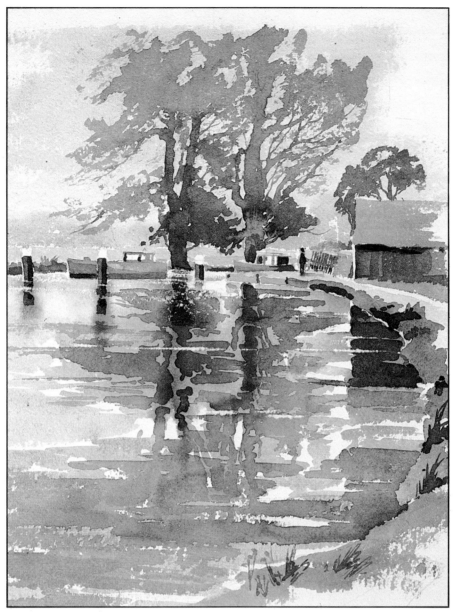

Finished stage   28 × 21cm (11 × 8¼in)

Third stage Now wet the paper again over the water area and, while it is still wet, run in the reflected colours. Before you start, decide roughly where they are going to be; for instance, the tree trunks, the red of the roof, and so on. I often have a dummy run over the paper with my brush to get the feel of where the strokes and colours will go. As you can see from this stage illustration, the colours merge and could even be left as finished. This, remember, was only the first wash but because the colours run into each other and the reflections and colours complement the background, to the eye it suggests water.

Finished stage When the first wash is nearly dry, add more, darker-colour washes and more, definite, reflection shapes to give more detail to the water. Finally, scratch out some horizontal highlights with a blade.

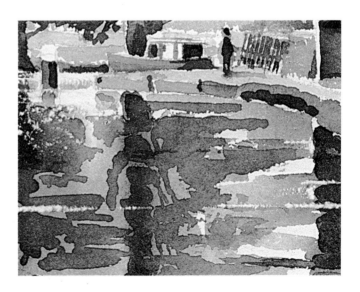

EXERCISE SEVEN
SNOW

In some parts of the world snow is never seen. It has a fascination all of its own: the stillness and quietness of a snowy landscape can be unbelievable. The clear rivers of the spring and summer turn to brown and the trees stand out in sharp silhouette.

One of the problems of painting snow is obvious – you can't take the family out for a picnic in six centimetres of snow, nor can you sit on the ground to paint. Above all, it is usually very cold. If you are going to paint snow out-of-doors, you must prepare yourself for nature's conditions. Always put on more clothing than you think you need – you can always take some off but you cannot go home for more. If you are carrying a sketch book, put it in a polythene bag so that it will stay dry if it is dropped in the snow. I once dropped mine in a pond – without polythene!

The best advice I can give you, when painting snow with watercolour, is to leave as much white paper as possible for snow. Snow is only white in its purest form, just fallen – and even then, it reflects light and colour from all around – but you need the white paper on which to add tone and colour reflections as you build up the painting. Add a little blue to cool the snow colour, or a little red or yellow to warm it up. Never be afraid to make snow dark in shadow areas. In comparison to its surroundings, it can be as dark as a shadow in a non-snow landscape.

First stage Draw the picture with an HB pencil. Then, wet the sky thoroughly with a sponge and, while it is still wet, paint it with your large brush and plenty of watery paint, using Payne's Grey, Crimson Alizarin and Yellow Ochre. Before this wash is completely dry, use the same colours, but stronger, to paint the distant trees with very broad, downward brush strokes, leaving the trunks of the main trees untouched.

Second stage Now, put in the three dark trees with your large, round brush, using French Ultramarine, Burnt Umber and Crimson Alizarin; work upwards to the top of the tree with a wet, loaded brush. Change to your size No. 6 brush while the paint is still wet and work on the small branches. Again, while these are wet, use your large brush a little drier and drag over the small branches – this gives the shape of the top of the trees. You will find that the paint runs into the branches in some areas and this is what you want. Work the nearest tree darker.

Third stage Start with the farthest trees on the left, using the same colours as before. Paint these very freely and very wet. As you work towards the centre, add Cadmium Yellow Pale, Yellow Ochre and Hooker's Green No. 1 to warm up the trees that still have some autumn leaves on them. Work these with your size No. 6 brush; keep the paint very wet all the time, allowing your small branches to run into each other and merge. When these are nearly dry, add some more distinct branches to bring these trees into focus and to pull the nearer ones away from the middle distance. Also, paint the end of the hut to the right of the main tree, using Cadmium Red and Yellow Ochre.

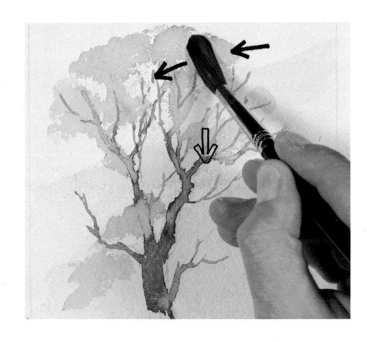

First stage

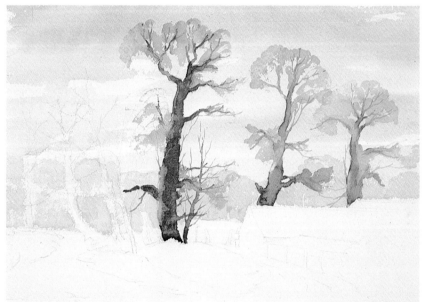

Second stage

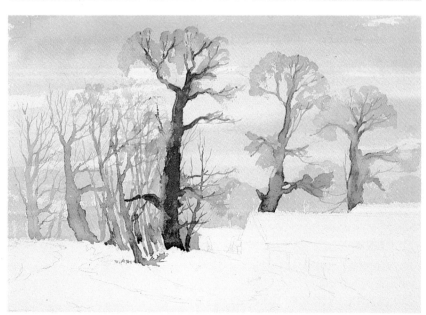

Third stage

55

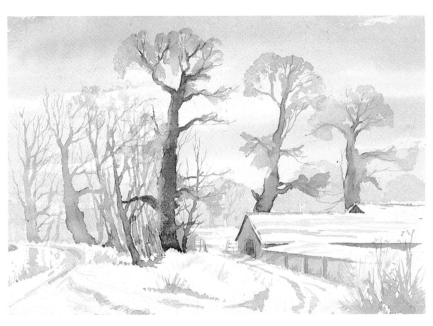

Fourth stage

Fourth stage Next, work on the buildings. Paint the top edge of the two buildings with Cadmium Red mixed with Cadmium Yellow Pale, using your size No. 6 brush. With the same colours put in the front wall of the nearest building, then add some French Ultramarine to your colour and paint the front of the main building (with the door). When this is dry, use the same colour, but darker, to suggest the door; paint the shadow under the gable and the building behind, to the right. Using the same colour, put in the shadow side of the main building (under the guttering). With the same brush and colour, draw the fence at the side of the building. Now you must put some moulding into the snow and path. Start by working on the ground that is not covered by snow; this is shown as ruts in the earth. Mix Crimson Alizarin, Yellow Ochre and Burnt Umber and use your size No. 6 brush to draw these shapes. Remember, the paper you leave unpainted will be snow. Paint the curve of the canal bank and, adding French Ultramarine to your colour, put in the reflections of the distant trees. With a

very wet brush mix Hooker's Green No. 1, Crimson Alizarin and French Ultramarine, work upwards with very free brush strokes and put in the grass and bramble at the bottom right of the picture. You will find that all the colours run together – this is intentional. Mix French Ultramarine and Crimson Alizarin, and paint the shadows on the snow-clad roofs of the buildings, also on the distant field.

Finished stage This is the stage that brings the picture to life. Using your large brush, mix French Ultramarine and Crimson Alizarin, and put in the shadows on the snow; keep the edges free and continue the main shadow from the large tree up the side of the wall and over the roof. Keep your colours wet and your brush strokes loose when you paint these shadows; look at the paper first, decide where you are going to paint them, then go ahead. Remember, if you cover up too much white paper, your snow will start to disappear or, at best, the sun will appear to have gone in. Now, put some more detail work into the large tree and the one to its left. Paint more small branches and dark accents where needed.

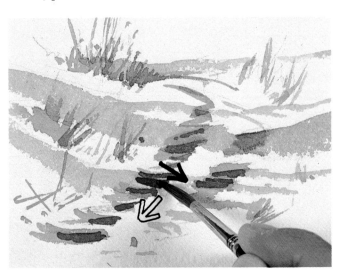

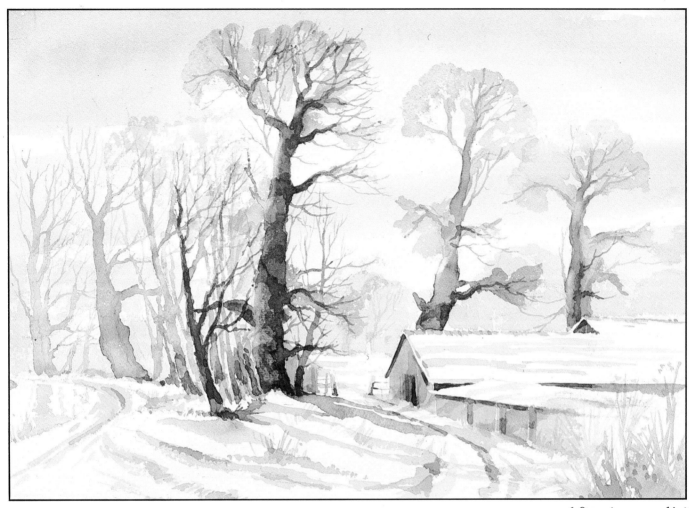

Finished stage

25.3×36.8cm ($10 \times 14\frac{1}{2}$in)

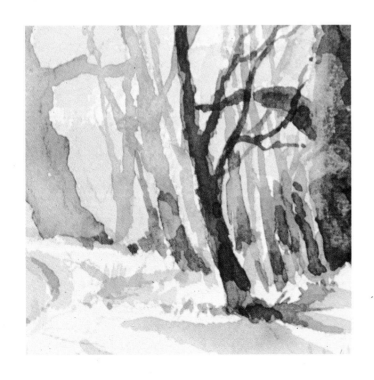

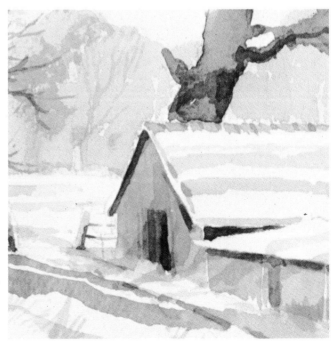

EXERCISE EIGHT
HARBOUR

Usually, artists who like painting the sea also enjoy painting harbours and boats. We feel very similar emotions when we are painting these three subjects but boats make one important difference – they make us feel more intimate with the sea, secure in the knowledge that life is around, especially in a harbour. In this painting of a harbour in Brittany, your next exercise, we can feel the intimacy of the scene: boats are everywhere, creating a feeling of activity, and the sun is dancing on the boats and water.

You need more knowledge of drawing to paint boats than to paint a landscape. For instance, if you paint a branch of a tree lower than the real one, it will still look right in your painting; but if you paint the mast of a boat at the wrong angle, then the painting will look obviously wrong. If possible, spend a few days sketching all the bric-a-brac, natural and unnatural, of a small harbour – from an old wreck sticking out of the mud like the backbone of a great fish, to an old piece of chain, all rusty and abandoned. You will acquire a tremendous amount of knowledge and an invaluable familiarity with boats and their surroundings.

This harbour scene was taken from a sketch; therefore, I had plenty of time to correct the drawing and make a careful study on the paper in the studio. If I had painted this outside, the drawing would have been looser and the painting would have been more impressionistic. Because of all the activity and the amount of drawing in the harbour, I decided to let you work this as a pen and wash drawing. Remember, this is a very sunny, summer afternoon – don't be afraid to use your colours.

First stage Use your HB pencil to draw the picture and make sure that the bottom edge of the harbour wall (i.e. the water level) is horizontal. Now use your large brush to paint a wash of Coeruleum Blue and Crimson Alizarin on the sky, adding more Crimson Alizarin and water as you near the roof tops. With your size No. 6 brush and a wash of French Ultramarine and Crimson Alizarin, paint the roof tops; add Cadmium Yellow Pale to the wash and paint the buildings. Let some of this colour (darker tones) also work as shadows on the buildings. Add some Hooker's Green No. 1 to this colour and paint the trees. Finally, adding more French Ultramarine to the same wash, paint the near side of the harbour wall, watering down the wash for the distant part.

Second stage Start working from the left-hand side of the houses with your size No. 6 brush to finish off the houses and little boats; use darker tones and suggest windows with just one brush stroke. Don't worry about too much neatness with your washes because the pen and ink will clean everything up and hold the picture together. As you work to the right of the buildings, make sure you put in the distinct shadows on the two square, white buildings. Then, let your brush wander along the quay and distant houses, making shapes and suggesting buildings. Work on the middle-distance boats with the colours shown; where you have a white boat use French Ultramarine and Crimson Alizarin for the shadow areas. Work these boats freely – do not get too involved in detail, this will be done by the pen – you are really going for form, expressed by colour and light and shade. For the woodwork on the boats use Burnt Sienna and French Ultramarine, working from the farthest boats to the nearest ones.

Third stage At this stage we are ready to paint the water. When you did this in the water exercise, you worked on wet paper. In this harbour scene *don't* wet the paper first – work on dry paper. Use your large brush, mix a wash of Coeruleum Blue and a little Crimson Alizarin – to reflect the sky colour – and be ready with the local colours of the boats. Now, start at the harbour wall and work down the painting. It is very important in this technique to leave *plenty of white paper showing*. Work the brush freely, in horizontal strokes, and add your boat-coloured reflections as you come to them. If the paint runs into another part of the water, let it; this helps to give more feeling to the area. Now, paint the flat stones on the edge of the harbour wall with French Ultramarine, Crimson Alizarin and Yellow Ochre; use your large brush and keep the strokes horizontal.

Fourth stage We have now arrived at the pen work. This can be done with various types of pen and using various treatments. You can use a felt-tip pen (fine point), a fountain pen with the right nib or, as I have, a mapping pen. The advantage of using a mapping pen is that you can draw a *very, very fine line*, which you cannot do with other pens. If you use a felt pen, you can make the stroke *down or up* the paper equally well but if you try this with a mapping pen and you use too much pressure or the paper has too much

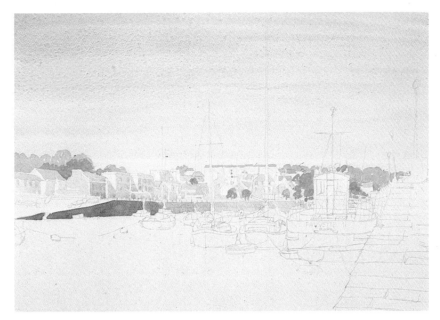

First stage

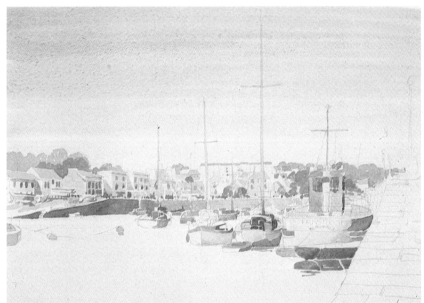

Second stage

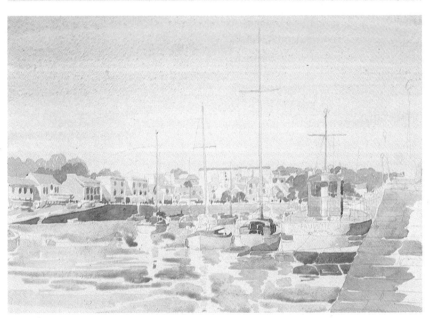

Third stage

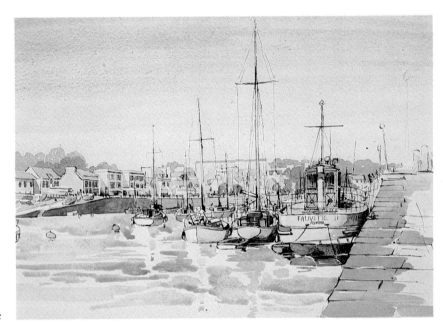

Fourth stage

tooth, on the up stroke it will bite into the paper and splatter your work with ink, and sometimes bend your nib. So, remember, the down stroke can be heavy but the up stroke must be lighter in pressure. Practise on some paper before going on to a painting and, as with your brushes, get used to your pens. Use black Indian waterproof ink. Now, start on the left of your picture, drawing the houses, windows, shutters, shadows under the eaves, and so on. Work into the distant houses and then use your pen very lightly to get thinner lines because these houses have to stay on the *other side* of the harbour. Now, work on the farthest boats in the harbour, giving them shape, and let the pen doodle a little here and there to give a complicated, crowded look in the middle distance. Remember, you are aiming for suggestion

in this area. Work forward, towards the nearest boats, putting in more detail as you near the quay wall. Draw the masts of the larger boats and some rigging. Suggest some stonework on the harbour wall on the right; your pen lines can now be stronger.

Finished stage The water is the last stage. Use your pen at a much flatter angle than for the boats and general work (see below). In the water example, the pen is held very low and makes horizontal strokes. These become thicker and looser than the other pen work. Still leave plenty of white paper. Finally, add any more accents or harbour paraphernalia with the pen. If you like (I didn't here), add a bit more colour or tone with paint if you think it will improve your work.

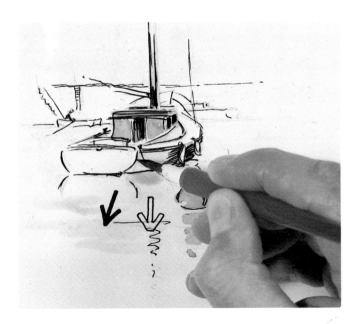

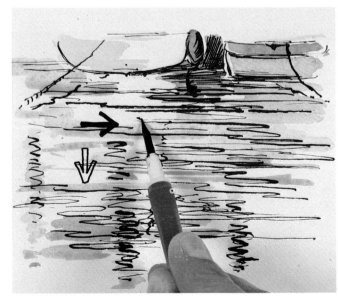

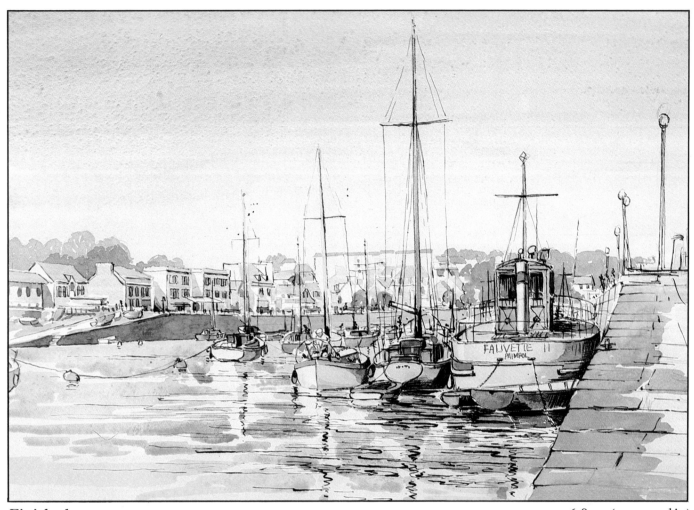

Finished stage   25.3 × 36.8cm (10 × 14½in)

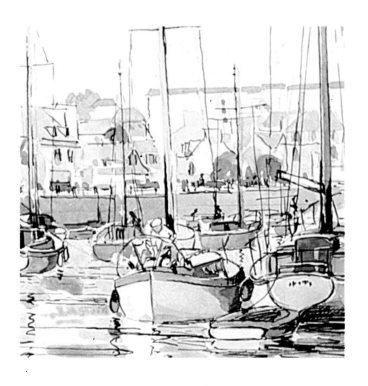

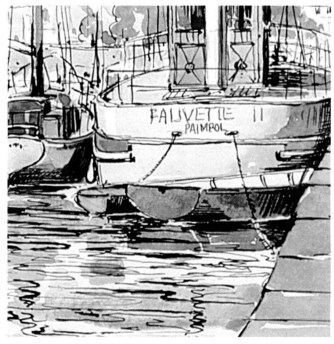

EXERCISE NINE
SEASCAPE

The sea has always fascinated artists. It has extremes of mood, from blissfully romantic to simply terrifying. Like the sky, the sea changes colour and, of course, it is always moving. This must be observed from life: sit on the beach and watch wave after wave coming in to learn how a wave is formed and how it breaks. Then, try sketching with a 3B pencil, concentrating on the overall form of the wave. Of course, you can't draw the same wave but there's another, and another, and another. You have to get a retained image to carry on to the next wave, carry that image on to the next, and so on. Then, you can try painting from life.

Remember that the horizon line must always be horizontal, otherwise the sea will appear to be falling off the paper; if necessary, draw it with a ruler. The sky must match the sea in colour and tone; in general, use the same colours for both. To give a seascape more interest we have cliffs, beaches, rocks and boats. Cliffs and headland give distance and perspective; beaches and rocks give us the opportunity to paint crashing waves and flying spray.

First stage I have taken this painting up to and including the third stage as a pure watercolour. In the final stage, I have continued and finished it in body colour. Basically, this is to demonstrate how, if you find you have lost the quality of a watercolour, you can add White to your colours and, perhaps, save your painting. Also this is another method of working a body colour painting. Start with watercolour washes then, when the painting is mapped out, add White and continue in body colour. (My previous body colour painting (page 26) was not done in this way, I added White to the colours at the start.) Now, wet your sky area thoroughly with water, *but not by the headland*, and paint the sky with your large brush, using Payne's Grey, French Ultramarine, Crimson Alizarin and Yellow Ochre. Use the same colours with a touch of Cadmium Yellow Pale to paint the far headland.

Second stage Paint the sea with Payne's Grey, French Ultramarine, Hooker's Green No. 1 and Crimson Alizarin, leaving white areas where the waves are breaking and using dry brush to get a sparkle on the water.

Third stage Paint the rocks, using Burnt Umber, French Ultramarine and Hooker's Green No. 1. Then, use your large brush to wet the beach and paint it in broad strokes, using the same colours as for the sea but adding Yellow Ochre. You will find the paint runs (wet on wet) to give some lovely, soft, watery effects.

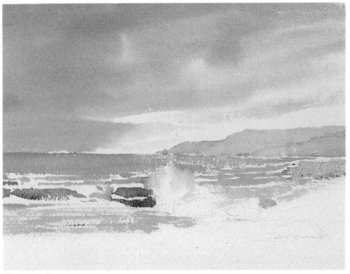

First stage

Second stage

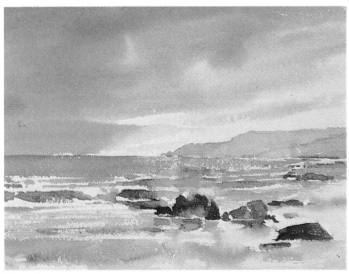

Third stage

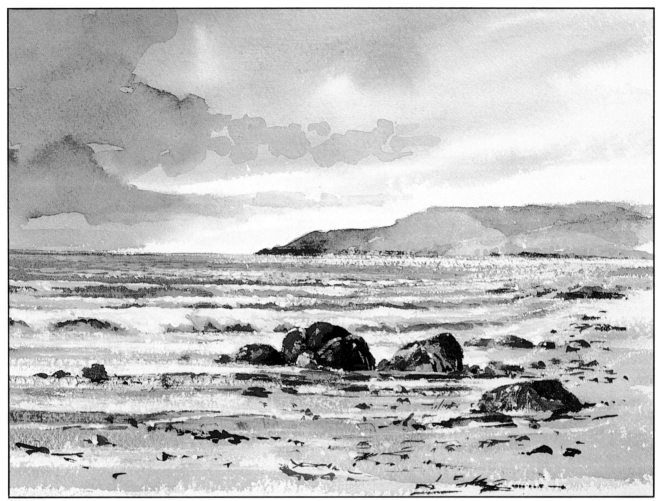

Finished stage   25.3 × 34cm (10 × 13⅜in)

Finished stage Before you add White to your colours, put another dark wash over the sky and sea. For the middle-distance sea use White with French Ultramarine and your size No. 6 brush; paint the waves (see centre illustration) and put the shadow cast by the heavy clouds on the head-land. Use almost pure White (add just a little Crimson Alizarin and Cadmium Yellow Pale) to form the large waves and darken them underneath to give shape and form. Darken the beach and, with dry brush technique, add White in horizontal strokes for the foam running up to the rocks. Now, add more rocks in the distance and let the brush draw some flotsam and jetsam on the beach. Add some white lines on the beach to create ripples of water and some lighter tones on the rocks to show sunlight. Remember, White is added to all the colours in this stage. This is a very popular technique but, like learning how to apply a wash for pure watercolour, you have to practise to get good results.

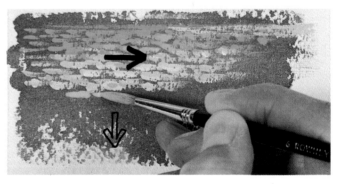

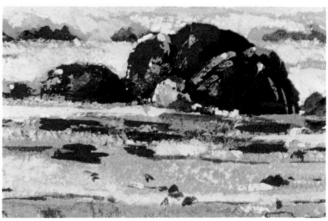